Non-Executive Directors

Non-Executive Directors

A guide to their role, responsibilities and appointment

KEN LINDON-TRAVERS

Published in association with the Institute of Directors

DIRECTOR BOOKS

Published by Director Books,
an imprint of Woodhead-Faulkner Limited,
Simon & Schuster International Group,
Fitzwilliam House, 32 Trumpington Street,
Cambridge CB2 1QY, England

First published 1990

The views of the author do not necessarily represent those of the Council of the Institute of Directors.

British Library Cataloguing in Publication Data
Lindon-Travers, Ken
Non-executive directors.
1. Great Britain. Companies. Non-executive directors. Role
I. Title II. Institute of Directors
658.4220941

ISBN 1–870555–11–2

Designed by Geoff Green
Typeset by Quorn Selective Repro Ltd
Printed in Great Britain by BPCC Wheatons Ltd, Exeter

This book is dedicated to the late
Angus Murray who was a model for other
non-executive directors to emulate.

This book is dedicated to my late [illegible] Murray, who was [illegible] director [illegible].

Contents

Preface

It is not just coincidence that some companies always find themselves in areas of growth and opportunity, whereas others are continually fighting for survival in yesterday's business fields. In essence, the difference lies in the quality and ability of their boards.

There is no doubt in the minds of business leaders that non-executive directors who are independent, properly selected and aptly used bring to a board skills and experience which are crucial in successfully directing the company. Many businessmen propose to increase numbers of non-executive directors to either a majority, on unitary boards, or the entire supervisory board, in a two-tier structure. Nevertheless, some still hold grave reservations about the practical value of the non-executive role, *per se*.

As long as such differences of opinion exist the non-executive story will remain unsuccessful. This book has several aims: to expand understanding of the role, its complex relationships and the situations in which a non-executive functions; to suggest ways in which a non-executive can contribute effectively; to examine alternative board concepts and, finally, to remove some of the mystical humbug which for years has diminished the ability of company boards in the United Kingdom.

Acknowledgements

The following people were prepared to interrupt their busy lives and contribute personal insights relating to the role of the non-executive director: without these comments the book would not be complete. I am most grateful to them all, and especially to Andrew Hutchinson who showed great resolution in reading the original draft.

Nicholas Bark
Pam Bater
Alan Binder OBE
George Bull OBE
John Chaloner
Tony Chubb
David Fraser
Kenneth Fraser
Andrew Hutchinson
The Rt. Hon. Aubrey Jones
David Hubbard
Gabs Kfouri
Philip Ling
Karen Morgan
Desmond Pitcher
Frank Ruheman
Henry Short
Douglas Strachan
Rab Telfer CBE
Roy Watts CBE
Kenneth Winckles MBE

1

Origins and Evolution

When and wherever business happens, people, power and risk taking will be close though not always harmonious companions, as they were even before the present concept of the limited company developed in the early 1850s.

Before the nineteenth century, merchant venturers financed their needs individually, or from within a kindred group, looking outside for a line of credit only as a means of last resort. They knew that such sponsors of capital weighed with skill and care the rigorous terms they demanded against a 'worst result possibility' – then added a little more for good measure. Many will ask: what has changed?

In contrast, the facility to draw upon the experience and sound judgement of others has long been valued, no less in business than in private life. The processes of comparing beliefs and perceptions, testing embryonic ideas and mentally measuring opportunities against limitations are natural functions within our society and, by consensus, will remain so.

What the creation of the company did was to introduce an additional element into the venturer–sponsor relationship. It created a quite separate entity, legally recognised, regulated and registered, with the capacity to act as a body apart from those who provided its capital. The company so formed limited the liability of its shareholders to the company's debts, reduced the risk factor and simultaneously enlarged the operating scope for people with power and enterprise in mind.

The late eighteenth and early nineteenth centuries also witnessed unprecedented growth in new railway, canal and construction projects associated with the industrial revolution. In both size and number, these ventures had an immense appetite for capital, and the development of the legal basis of the company went *pari passu* with the physical development, culminating in the Acts of 1855, limiting the liability of members of certain joint-stock companies, and 1862, which established rules for the formation of an incorporated company and the preparation of its Memorandum of Association.

However, although these developments partially underwrote security and thereby encouraged a host of new sources for capital, the Acts could not and did not reduce investors' risk of incurring losses as a result of either their limited knowledge of the business or their inability to supervise those who managed its affairs.

It is perhaps worth noting that this burgeoning investor era happened some seventy years ahead of the very restricted protection framework introduced through the Securities and Exchange Commission in the United States, and almost a century and a half in advance of the necessary, but quite radical, regulatory reforms which are being implemented by the Security and Investment Board in the United Kingdom today.

In their wisdom, however, the devisers of the Acts once again provided a simple and expedient solution by requiring companies to appoint directors, as against managers, not only to supervise their operations but also, at regular intervals, to report to the investors/shareholders their understanding of past events, future plans and the current financial status of the business. These reports were to be suitably qualified or audited by an independent professional accountancy practice. The role of these directors was non-executive.

DIRECTORS WERE LOCAL

The businesses which developed in those times were for the most part utilising labour, energy and material resources which were readily available either in the immediate geographical area or from a major port nearby. It naturally followed that shareholders chose to elect as their directors people of some prominence in the local community, or in the city which housed the central control of the company. A knowledge of affairs, commercial experience, integrity and influence were sought-after qualities, and someone of professional status added credibility to the company and a degree of comfort for investors.

The power of individual ownership was strong, since pension funds were not in existence and institutional investors were uncommon. It was individuals, banking houses and small speculative syndicates which backed an enterprise, taking a positive interest in its activities and expecting their supporting role to continue in the long term. Computer-programmed share dealing was beyond imagination, and the prospect that individual holdings in UK companies might one day fall below twenty-five per cent was totally unthinkable.

Apart from in the proprietorial company where, as today, the three roles often overlapped, ownership, direction and management were quite as distinct as the points of a triangle. A general manager, who was not a director, headed the team running day-to-day operations, a practice now only followed in the United Kingdom by a minority of building societies and financial institutions. The earliest version of Table A of the Companies Act 1985 (the statutory model articles of association) precluded directors from holding any employment or place of profit in the company.

THE UNITARY BOARD

As the turn of the century approached, and as many established commercial and industrial businesses turned themselves into public limited companies, their board composition began to change. Managers, and previous owners with their technical know-how, initimate understanding of the business, and practical control over the implementation of decisions, held a combination of power factors which, if not determining, could have a major influence on results – and results mattered.

The title 'managing director' became as frequently associated with the promoted executive achiever as it was with the founding entrepreneur. Functional director appointments soon followed and those without full-time executive roles declined in numbers as well as authority, with only the holding of significant share stakes or personal relationships ensuring a board seat to individuals who did not work full time in the company. What is known today as the unitary board was established.

This unitary concept will be used in later chapters as the scenario in which most UK company non-executives now make their contribution and will be compared against European and North American alternatives. This suggests neither exclusivity nor merit; however, in spite of increasing EC pressure for the introduction of a two-tier system and a positive evolutionary change in that direction, the unitary board is likely to predominate in the United Kingdom at least until 1995, which opens the door for considerable speculation as to the future.

PERFORMANCE IN DECLINE

It may have been sheer coincidence and not a contributing factor that executive dominance in UK boardrooms happened at about the time that effective direction of industrial and commercial companies began to wither. But common sense suggests that not to acknowledge a positive connection between the two events would be a case of flagrant self-deception.

In the two decades following the First World War other related issues emerged. The absence of a national will to accept change, to modernise or invest in the future, was in sharp contrast to the polarisation of political doctrines and the emergence of organised labour unions. Together, these provided untrodden territory on which to test the qualities of business leaders.

The response was apathetic, too readily reflecting the national mood. After all, labour, food and housing were cheap, and the 'tied trade' market of the Empire was still in existence, its agreements negotiated with the assistance of a loaded gun. Credit was good and traditional reputations were still high, so what was the urgency?

Certainly the pressures failed to come from shareholders, whose rights of ownership and exercise of power became a permanent mirage. Annual meetings mostly degenerated into sparsely attended rituals where the primary objective appeared to be the continuance of the board rather than that of the company.

This strange and unnatural cultural evolution therefore continued beyond another war and into the gradual dissolution of imperial trading links. UK companies, long since outpaced in productivity and contribution to GDP by those of North America, were now being outclassed by the French and West Germans in Europe, and the rising sun of more onerous competition was just appearing in the East.

As younger people deserted the business or commercial career path in favour of more comfortable and socially acceptable routes towards their personal goals, companies short of imagination and vitality remained under the governance of boards which had become institutionalised to the point of being ossified of mind and slothful in corporate body, boards which were still entrenched in yesterday's business and unprepared for the opportunities of tomorrow.

LIVING IN YESTERYEAR

The style of non-executives during these years was characteristic of this process in reflecting the 'good old days' of the past: a retired admiral, an ex-diplomat or a politician here, an overcommitted industrial giant, a City banker or a 'professional non-executive' there, all bringing an outward credibility to the board by their presence but able to do little else. As one chairman commented, such non-executives were no more than 'a nice assembly of names to have on the annual report'.

Few non-executives were appointed from sources other than a list of former executives or the chairman's particular circle of friends and acquaintances, and total board involvement in selection was an exceptional and unusual democratic occasion. An air of mysticism surrounded both nomination processes and the people concerned in them, and many board members still found the events inexplicable even after the appointment was made. A now-retired chief executive recalled of his non-executives, 'They always listened attentively to the problems, they smiled, they nodded, but all they ever said was "good luck to you", then wafted away in a cloud of importance.' It was thought, and too often still is, that just by being there the non-executive contribution was fulfilled.

Calls for change in the system of self-perpetuating hierarchy were kindly presented and a guiding article in *The Director* in 1972 said:

> There has been a spate of books lately on management, good, bad and indifferent. Managers have seen themselves compared with feudal barons, heads of state, religious leaders, and apes. This has made for stimulating controversy and may even have some effect on management performance. But directors, meanwhile, can feel neglected. They may breathe a thankful sigh of relief for that. Nonetheless they would be foolish to ignore the new thinking that is going on, on the Continent, in America and in Britain itself, about the role of the board in a rapidly changing world and about the performance and responsibility of directors in an era of sharply increasing social and economic challenge.

But despite the warnings, as the economic and competitive challenges built up in the 1970s, company after company of long tradition and great national standing crumpled, 'core elements' of their businesses disappeared and the fragmented remains became unviable. The directors had patently failed to navigate them through the 'Bermuda Triangle of business'.

THE NON-EXECUTIVE MANDATE

In these circumstances, what degree of responsibility should the non-executive bear? Sir Kenneth Cork in his foreword to the Institute of Director's Code of Practice, commented as follows:

> [Non-executives] are the people to whom the auditors talk . . . they are the people who should assess impartially the ability of management . . . they are the people who should be prepared to stand up and be counted . . . if they fail in their duties then their 'licence' to be a non-executive should be withdrawn.

These comments are sometimes thought to be unjustified as non-executives frequently felt that they were, or should be, above criticism because they were not directly accountable for running the business. Nevertheless we continue to witness companies foundering in both advantageous and difficult economic circumstances, notwithstanding their boards being able to boast a full 'quota' of so-called non-executives. In total they represent an indictment of ineffectual presence against all who assume the non-executive mantle, and they pass ammunition to those who would rather run the board with no independent representation around the table.

Some may feel these critical views of the non-executive director to be unjust and too harsh. After all, they may claim, in the time available non-executives could not really be expected to know much about the business or the way it is managed – and events happen so quickly. Not a particle of such a defence is plausible. Detailed knowledge of the business is not crucial, but knowing about business, about its effective direction and management, most certainly is. Decline and disaster reflect months if not years of neglect and muddled thinking. Non-executives should not allow themselves to be subject to internal pressures or conflicts of personal interest or ambition; their primary reason for existence is to direct the company away from threats and dangers and towards opportunities for successful continuance and growth. Forward thinking and appreciation of the time scales involved is part of that responsibility.

CHANGE OF MOOD AND TEMPO

As the 1980s began, there were three sound causes for optimism. Firstly, irrepressible entrepreneurs kept emerging in corporate vehicles large and small, devising new rules for the business game and exploiting them to great advantage. Their sensors were tuned to reshaping business portfolios, rethinking strategies and creating innovative enterprise concepts. With or without formal boards, the high-risk, high-pay-off adventure has always attracted enough players to build a dynamic momentum. Once a commercial venture is generating profit and looks set for quite rapid growth, an entrepreneur's options are either to sell his shareholding to make a quick personal profit, or to manage the business on a long-term basis through continued development – the objective then being to create a major company. Although riding a corporate roller-coaster is perhaps more exhilarating, it is primarily in the latter instance that non-executives play a most useful part.

Secondly, government was beginning to undermine entrenched attitudes and release people's minds from inflexible beliefs in the established rights of their own particular sacred cows. Traditional markets, margins, demarcation lines, protection, subsidies and lame-duck rescue acts for sheer political expediency could no longer be taken for granted. The days of reckoning had arrived. Outmoded businesses in outdated markets closed their doors forever – being management no longer assured job protection. Survival demanded change, soft options disappeared.

Thirdly, the enduring leaders of the business community, who by their foresight and adept judgement had largely ridden out the recession, were now joined by a band of seasoned survivors and ambitious first-time achievers. Together they determined to promote a new realism in direction and management, and to meet head-on the 'British disease'. In countless small and large companies, objectives and priorities became clearer and disciplines tighter as the principles of the 'right to manage' and the 'duty to manage properly' were reintroduced. One by one, industry leaders stood up to be counted, with businesses in the steel, printing, automobile, coal, shipping, chemicals and construction industries setting the pace. The City, at the same time, revitalised its catalytic role with such impetuosity that it almost moved out of control. Self regulation was proving inadequate, new regulatory bodies such as Securities and Investment Board (SIB) were not in place and existing forms of policing, the Department of Trade and Industry (DTI) for example, were outclassed.

These three key elements found enough common ground to boost UK economic performance levels above those of its European and North American competitors and, after an interval of almost a century, to re-establish the United Kingdom as a wealth-creating nation.

A NEED FOR PROFESSIONALISM

As neglected companies were decimated and their boards were inflicted with a similar fate, an unusual volume of outspoken criticism was directed at the establishment and old-style non-executives. This was not without good reason since, although it is an impossible task to quantify performance, few might question the supposition that in the main their input was substandard.

It would, however, be manifestly wrong to suggest that most non-executive directors acted other than in good faith, and worse to attempt to brand them all as incompetent freeloaders. They were supposed to help provide the answers but, with scant understanding of their role and near-feudal allegiance to their patrons, in practice they seldom even understood the questions.

As yet, the position of director does not require either a professional qualification in company direction or is a 'licence' to practise, but pressure for both exists and is growing. Their introduction may eventually happen, perhaps within five to seven years if a champion emerges to lead the cause.

Such moves towards establishing professional standards would lend support to the Stock Exchange rule which stipulates that the board of any company seeking a listing should include a number of directors who are non-executive – usually at least two. Sadly, the Stock Exchange rule is still half-hearted on other counts: it fails to specify independence or even to advise how such non-executive directors can be genuinely defined; and it shrinks away from imposing a minimum ongoing non-executive requirement – once quoted, a public limited company is at liberty to dispense with some or all of its non-executives without regard to replacement.

Although two-tier boards, or a UK version of them, are the crucial talking point for tomorrow, today's consensus is clearly in favour of the unitary system with its blending of inside and outside directors. The judicious balancing of the board complement is positively encouraged by both the Institute of Directors and the Promotion of Non-Executive Directors (PRO NED), whose initiatives not only promote wider understanding and use of the non-executive but also mastermind the supply of sound advice and suitable people.

In spite of such goodwill, effective contributors remain scarce. The influx of potential recruits resulting from board-room shake-outs has done little to alleviate this shortage, for most are either already rapidly distancing themselves from the scene of activity or, as directors, are well past their 'sell-by' dates.

In contrast, an almost welcome reduction in the numbers of volunteers resulted from the passing of the Insolvency Act in 1985. Its deterrent element gave rise to some rapid rethinking by both casual opportunists and those tempted into a paid part-time occupation which, when cleverly worked, was low in personal demands, actual participation and eventual responsibility. The Act is now beginning to take effect, and by 1990 some 750 cases of alleged improper conduct by directors will have been reviewed, the vast majority resulting in penalties which include disqualification for between two and fifteen years.

FULL CIRCLE

In this way, within little more than a century, the rationale of the non-executive has moved full circle. Initially, the non-executive was a person with almost unfettered discretion and responsibility to direct management of a company in the owners' interests. Then the non-executive role became that of a weak and near-ineffectual partner to the burgeoning full-time executives, together looking either backwards or inwards, but seldom forwards. Finally, albeit gradually and with considerable prompting, the non-executive began to return to a role which carries evident responsibility and accountability in law.

2

Non-Executive Directors and the Company

Just as companies differ one from another in structure, objectives, standards and culture, so the input each needs from its non-executives will differ – as indeed will the personal qualities and weight of the non-executives themselves. To gain at least some firm footholds in this morass of variables, simple characteristics of size and style have been used to create identifiable groups against which to relate the non-executive role.

The availability and accuracy of information on the variables of company size, number and activity are only marginally better than they are of the non-executive directors who help direct their affairs. At the top end, public limited companies (plcs) and the larger private companies are well documented on both counts. Information is fragmented in the middle and smaller company ground, while in the vast residual rump of very small private/sunrise companies any statistics produced from statutory records are invariably overtaken and outdated by events. So, in order to present a broad picture of the current scene, a degree of presumption is perhaps permissible.

In number, registered and active UK companies total about 450,000, that figure excluding dormants, terminal cases or those in the process of formation. The bulk, over 60 per cent, are in the small sunrise classification, while about one-third are either subsidiaries or joint ventures. The balance, a minuscule two and a half to three per cent, represent the eleven thousand, or so plcs and private companies which have an annual turnover in excess of £3 million. It is this last group which attracts the lion's share of attention both from non-executives and in the following chapters of this book, their boards having the ultimate decision-making responsibility for over 95 per cent of all UK industrial and commercial activity.

SUNRISE COMPANIES

The multitude of very small businesses and sunrise ventures are not left aside through lack of importance but principally because in companies with sales of less than £3 million it is unusual to find either a formal management structure or directors who are invited to attend regular board, as distinct from management, meetings. Many may exclaim with great feeling that the same can be said for the larger groups – but that is a subject to which we shall return later.

> **Comment**
> 'It's the presence of the non-executive director which makes a board meeting a board meeting, not a management or committee meeting.'

Few dispute the claim that a non-executive is better able to ensure that the value of his or her wider viewpoint and experience is available to co-directors when a form of agenda is followed, no matter how informal the circumstances. If asked to join a very small company, a non-executive should consider as a primary task the guidance of colleagues in the gradual introduction and establishment of some meetings when longer-term plans and matters of policy and direction are the keynotes.

Sunrise companies are a vital part of any economy, not least because of their growth potential, and support should be given to them without undue interference. Under their typical owner/manager control, they have no less need than a larger company for the input of an experienced and independent outsider, especially one who is still youthful in mind. If anything, their need is even greater because in these situations a non-executive's contribution should include an element of coaching which, by practical example, will aid the perception and development of director skills in both the boss and the other top people.

Frequently, before budding companies have any formal structure, this deficit in objective know-how is met not through the appointment of a non-executive director, but rather through the availability of wise counsel and commercial advice provided quite informally by a friend, professional adviser or a multi-role freelance businessman – or all three combined in one. Such guru relationships are an everyday fact of life in business and are in no way unique to this size of company. In addition to their use of non-executive directors, many chairmen and chief executives of medium and large companies set great store by a private mentor behind the scenes.

Aspiring industry leaders should not underestimate the very real benefits for them and their companies of a personal adviser who is a seasoned director and who can, when necessary, provide relevant business experience. However, great caution should be used in choosing a particular guru, in order to avoid the smooth-talking, well-connected ne'er-do-well, to resist the temptation to use friends under a convenient guise, and not to get locked into a long-term arrangement which began in a spate of overenthusiasm.

The facility of being able to tap into a pool of talent and experience is crucial to the successful growth of many small and sunrise companies, and this will be an important feature of Chapter 10.

THE MAJOR CORPORATIONS

It is perhaps surprising to know that over 80 per cent of total UK business volume is generated under the control of no more than one thousand main company boards, albeit with a multitude of subsidiary and joint-venture companies below. These majors, of which over 90 per cent are plcs, have annual turnovers in excess of £100 million each and on occasions develop a group structure with ten or more levels, the top fifty having spawned upwards of ten thousand companies as subsidiaries. The ultimate decisions, however, rest with that small core of people who are generally referred to as group directors or, collectively, as the board.

Board size, averaging between nine and ten people, has an unusually wide span; it is seldom less than seven but rises to well above twenty in some banks and financial institutions. Generally, the top one hundred companies have larger boards but their median does not exceed twelve.

Composition presents some interesting features with only the exceptional company not including non-executives on its board. Numerically, executives dominate in eight out of ten instances, the balance being split between boards where non-executives and executives are equal and those where non-executives predominate. Non-executives normally account for one in three main board directors, though there are now signs that the proportions are beginning to change with the number of non-executives slowly increasing.

Two illustrative contrasts in size and composition have been subjects of successful flotations in recent years. The TSB board, after its acquisition of Hill Samuel, rose in number to a staggering thirty, which comprised the chairman, deputy chairman, managing director, seven executive directors and twenty other directors, eight of whom were appointed for their specialist knowledge and experience and twelve with regional connections; non-executive directors appeared to be an unknown species. It was interesting to note how Sir Nicholas Goodison, when appointed chairman in 1989, upheld his long-standing commitment to the wider use of non-executives in his previous role as chairman of the Stock Exchange, quickly introducing drastic cuts to existing board numbers and bringing in independent outsiders.

The board of British Airways, which at the time had a similar operating profit, found ten members sufficient, comprising the chairman, Lord King, a deputy chairman, chief executive, chief financial officer and six non-executives. The corporate BA board, although smaller, is quite similar in style to the board composition found in most North American companies, where non-executives fill ten seats in an average board total of thirteen – virtually a reverse ratio to current practice in the UK. BA also favours the trend towards promoting a strong executive management board, with each of the thirteen incumbents using the prefix title 'Director of ', and the chief executive and the financial officer linking policy to executive management by sitting on both boards. This arrangement has the distinction of combining a 'policy direction' board with one targeted to 'executive operations', and it demonstrates a practical and progressive variation on the European two-tier system, where a totally non-executive senior board carries out a purely supervisory function.

An interesting but separate quandary faced the giant National Westminster Bank. Its chairman, the appropriately named Lord Boardman, presided over a flock of thirty-one directors, a number almost bound to ensure a loss of contact with events. As his three score and ten years indicated approaching retirement, the company faced two problems. The first was to find an able successor when, for reasons discussed later, there was a dearth of skilled candidates. The second, and perhaps more difficult, was to find someone who would also be prepared to inherit the existing board size, style and composition. Together they presented the ultimate dilemma. Not surprisingly, one or two outstanding people reportedly found the chairmanship offer to be one they could easily refuse. The eventual choice was Lord Alexander of Weedon, previously chairman of the Take-over Panel, whose experience and ability as a formidable advocate will perhaps add a unique flair and style to his use of a chairman's baton.

At about the same time Lord Weinstock, whose GEC never seems to be found wanting for an adept chairman, was providing an amazing demonstration of speed and agility in the international acquisition, merger and joint-venture arena. As chief executive, he described his six non-executive directors as being 'independent both financially and personally' and maintained that the primary duty of non-executive directors was to see that 'the management of a company is competent and honest and that interests of shareholders are not traduced'. The GEC board is also patently international, which brings us to the next area of concern.

Internationalism

Most major corporations accept that companies should foster close relationships with universities to aid the introduction and use of skills in management sciences and advanced technology. Recruiting a non-executive from academia is now considered as much a part of the evolutionary process as drawing upon the latent talents in the public sector.

However, thought still to be revolutionary are the initiatives taken by some chairmen whose colleagues have fully endorsed some quite radical changes to the complement and balance of their boards in order to bring them into closer line with the company's objectives and strategy. These boards reflect their global business activities within the boardroom by introducing into their non-executive ranks prominent figures from the international industrial and commercial world.

Such a figure is Charles Price, former US Ambassador to the United Kingdom, who was readily invited to join the boards of Hanson, The New York Times, Texaco and British Airways. About the same time his wife, Carol Ann Price, became a director of the Savoy Hotel Group. That consistent trendsetter ICI followed the appointment of a leading Japanese industrialist, Shoichi Saba, by inviting Paul Volcker to join its board. This former chairman of the US Federal Reserve is considered one of the world's most distinguished bankers and obviously has an immense contribution to make to that board's viewpoint on financial and general international issues – quite apart from giving independently minded advice of the highest order.

This move towards multinational boards, pioneered by BOC among others, is firmly gathering pace and is perhaps moving too quickly for the specialist non-executive search firms to meet demand. Within a few years it may not seem extraordinary if the majority of companies which plan overseas trade in excess of £50 million are following a policy of appointing at least one non-executive director who is a foreign national and is not resident in the United Kingdom. This broader non-executive input provides a unique assessment of a company's international activities, threats and opportunities as seen from a different geographical base, industry background and management culture.

The US scene is typical in that, to an expansion-minded UK board, it represents a new business market of enormous potential in what at first appears to be a familiar cultural and commercial environment. It is not referred to as the 'first timer's graveyard' without just cause – two years on and a few million dollars lighter, it is too late to exchange tales of woe with other chairmen whose companies also learned to trade there the hard and costly way.

Hanson plc seems to manage the Atlantic bridge with consumate ease, and Michael Montague, chairman of Valor, planned his attack with thoroughness when in 1986 he recruited Bob Olney, a non-executive director with wide US experience. A year or so later, his transatlantic foray led to the successful acquisition of Yale and NU Tone, which changed Valor's standing overnight. Recently he has again demonstrated his internationalism by transferring production of the group's Dreamland products from Southampton to Oporto in Portugal.

UK companies now face the challenge of the Single European Market. If they are to compete effectively in the market-place of Europe, UK companies must have a board which understands how that market thinks and operates.

THE MIDDLE GROUND

Some five thousand companies, with turnovers ranging from £10 million to £100 million, comprise what are considered by many experienced non-executive directors to be the most exciting and rewarding businesses to join, their size being below the slower-moving formalities of the major corporations yet above the frustrations encountered in achieving 'lift-off' with the comparative minors. Certainly these companies are seldom short of problems to tax the resources of their outside directors.

Over the whole spectrum, non-executive directors average about a quarter of the board. However, there appears to be a curious upward popularity curve in the £20 million to £50 million segment when, according to statistics, the non-executive to executive ratio shows a marked increase. One possible reason for this feature might be a shift in the boardroom power base which occurs at certain stages during growth. As a company emerges from the 'small' category, the intuitive flair and dominance exercised by the founding family or entrepreneur becomes subject to new pressures and, although managerial competence may be stretched towards its limits, passing over direct control remains an unacceptable alternative that might be considered an admission of personal failure. At the same time, executive colleagues of long standing too often prove to be woefully short of experience in helping tackle the problems of building for tomorrow.

The need for change is evident and one of these three options is usually favoured:

- Find people who have 'been there before' to bring instant strength and experience in a non-executive capacity within a unitary board. Friends or business acquaintances are closely scrutinised and, increasingly, agencies like PRO NED or the Institute of Directors are used to widen both scope of search and choice. A more effective board normally results, but as the company grows some of the original executive directors cannot keep pace. In this case, changes have to be made to maintain both a balance of ability in the boardroom and between a board's expectation and the executives' capacities to deliver.
- Grasp the nettle and appoint a professional managing director to run the business, being mindful of course to ensure that he or she knows where and by whom the decisions are really made – or better still, always

being around to make them. The results are quite predictable.

- Examine a form of two-tier system which allows the founder's or family interests to be preserved through a policy board and at the same time gives a full measure of executive freedom for the managing director and the management board in running day-to-day operations.

The first two options are such everyday occurrences that they are almost taken for granted as part of a company's growing pains. The latter is often effected through the formation of a holding company and subsidiary boards, which is an unnecessary complication.

> **Comment**
> 'Dealing with crisis and disaster is in many ways easier than handling success, for then options and opportunities multiply. That's when a board's ability to make the right decisions is so crucial.'

This period of challenging growth is probably the most fruitful time for the 'outsiders' to show their paces, not least in helping to change the composition and balance of power within the board. Non-executive directors increase, executives decrease and, where wisdom prevails, the combined chairman/chief executive role is split. When this happens, as it frequently does, the chairman's role, albeit part time, needs to be recognised as being too important to be filled by someone who is already well on the way towards retirement and is only looking to fill a few respectable and untroubled years before bowing out altogether.

In this way, an era of a new-style direction comes into being, happening as readily within a private company as a plc and even in family-dominated versions of both. Complacency, however, takes root faster than chickweed and, after the initial turbulent years, savouring the fruits of success is an easy and comfortable habit to acquire. Almost as quickly, preserving the status quo becomes a matter of personal security.

All company activities are normally subject to some regular form of performance review – except those of the board. Deciding who might be recognised as suitably impartial for such a delicate task is a difficult enough question to answer even before broaching the subject of to whom the findings should be presented. External consultants might baulk at what would for them be a hearsay dominated brief whereas non-executive directors are clearly well positioned for such a task and, if their numbers are enough to form a 'critical mass', they are also best able to bring a weight of independent judgement and wide experience into their comments and recommendations. When this happens, the board continues to evolve as a living entity, reshaping itself to deal effectively with the future; when this fails to happen the board becomes just a reflection of the past.

> **Comment**
> 'It is not just coincidence that some boards of directors always seem able to steer their company into a position where it can exploit new areas of opportunity, while other companies continually find themselves trying to overcome the constraints and problems of being locked into yesterday's business.
>
> With few exceptions, the essential difference lies not in either a degree of luck or coincidence but in the quality and effectiveness of the board.'

Most board members have been aware of, or have played a part in, prime examples of both.

Whether or not a company is in a highly technical field makes little difference to its need for effective direction. Best growth in low-technology businesses usually comes when they are of middling size, perhaps during the second generation of their development, and when they are subjected to a vigorous input of new professionalism in strategic concepts, marketing and management drive. By the same token, companies in advanced technology must balance their natural emphasis on matters technical with a continual need to improve management skills.

It is, of course, easier to see these events in retrospect, but if non-executive directors are to earn their salt in these middle-range companies they must, more than any other director, exercise their minds on such issues. The great danger is that a boardroom seat tends to shape itself in a comfortable fashion as the years pass, especially when the duration of its tenancy was by default omitted from discussions at the time of appointment and talk of departure might now be a source of embarrassment.

Keeping the board highly tuned and flowing in creative business talent is therefore unquestionably one of the chairman's key objectives, and one to which the non-executive directors should make a valuable input. The alternative is likely to be a frustrating and bumpy ride as a company bounces along the route to major status.

THE SMALL COMPANY

Admittedly, among the five thousand companies in this group, a number of directors might feel aggrieved at being termed 'small' when, by any standards, a turnover between £3 million and £10 million is no mean business achievement. However, these lines are drawn to indicate the different forms in which the non-executive director's contribution is made, and in this group there are marked differences.

About half of these companies have non-executives and a fair proportion of those who do so either receive them as part of an inheritance, or just have these outsiders thrust upon them by people or companies who either hold a significant shareholding or are providers of finance.

In the battle to keep a business growing, the last thing an entrepreneurial managing director wants to face is the prospect of taking part in some sedate ritual in a boardroom, with a number of comparative strangers who do not understand what is going on and take up too much executive time on basic explanations. Of greater appeal is the prospect of coming to an informal advisory arrangement with a seasoned executive who has plenty of company experience and can act as an objective sounding board. This might even be seen as an act of liberation compared to existing close ties of family, founding colleagues and local advisers. Some or all of these may be directors who have contributed well in the past – but at a time when the company was really small.

Finding a non-executive who can eliminate all the factors of commercial risks which follow from decision making or external threats which may endanger a company's prospects is an unrealistic hope. The last mistake, or the last two or three, may have proved expensive and set the company development plan back several months. Although unfortunate, this is a matter of history. Now the objective is to reduce the probability of repetition through the introduction of a non-executive director who, amongst other qualities, has a well-honed commercial mind and a nose for sensing trouble.

The overriding incentive for a small company to use non-executives is to enlist help in keeping 'bottom line' results moving fast and upwards through the often perilous growth stages. The aim is to find someone who understands the business and has also been where the company intends to go, especially if that means passing through City boundaries *en route* to the Unlisted Securities Market (USM) or an alternative listing.

Complementary commercial or financial skills, larger company disciplines and a capacity to respond to the more immediate threats and opportunities combine to create the basic non-executive director profile in greatest demand for today's small business. When contributing to companies of this size, non-executives who know their job will not impose themselves on what is patently a management meeting in an attempt to give it a pseudo board connotation; nor will they promote either the frequency or duration of meetings in order to give themselves a platform on which to perform.

The capacity to create an effective small company board is one of a chairman's fundamental but least publicised talents, and the rarity of such people 'in house' is one reason why companies look outside for someone who already has experience in the role and can be available part time. Changing a board's composition is neither easy nor fast, especially in a small, close-knit business where some of the executives are also past their prime. Having a chairman who can exercise the necessary skills is crucial. The alternative is to continue facing yesterday and be likely to grind to a standstill in the process.

SUBSIDIARIES

With numbers over 100,000, these ubiquitous enterprises have in common at least a 51 per cent single parentage. That apart, they are found throughout business, include companies of private and plc status, and in size may range from a minute agency to a major international trader.

Except in rare cases, subsidiaries do not have the freedom of self-determination. In the eyes of most non-executive directors, when final decision making lies with the parent and is outside subsidiary boardroom control the opportunities to contribute are restricted and their role is consequently of less significance.

But this is not always so, for closer examination shows widely differing interpretations of the non-executive director's role. For example, UK subsidiaries of US or European parents often appoint both part-time chairmen and non-executives who are independent in every sense. Usually of British nationality, they are expected to present forthright opinions both at meetings in this country and from time to time when invited to join in discussions with the parent board. The exercise of independent judgement is then seen as critical to their value as non-executive directors.

In subsidiaries of UK parents, both executives and non-executives alike are seldom given the same latitude in devolved responsibility and decision making. For the most part, non-executive directors are drawn from the ranks of main board directors or senior functional executives of the same company and, although shown as non-executive on paper, carry out a quasi communications and watchdog function. Frequently when a number of directors duplicate their role on both subsidiary and parent board the whole structured process becomes something of a time-wasting nonsense.

As a result of these uncertainties, the discriminating independent non-executive director will often decline an approach to join the board of a subsidiary, time understandably being too valuable when scope is limited. The ready volunteers who have almost unlimited time on their hands can become a threat in their own right (see Chapter 3).

JOINT VENTURES

The joint venture is a widely used formula where either two equal sharing owners or a number in multi-ownership combine their separate industry or national interests into a larger single and hopefully harmonious entity. Often a UK company will not be allowed to hold more than 49 per cent of a joint venture when its partner is foreign-owned and the base of operations is in the partner's country. In many instances therefore the technical or commercial promoter has to accept this as the only deal available.

Whoever the participants may be, it appears almost naïve to assume that the parties can simply set up an operating company together with its appointed executives, each add two or three directors of their own under a non-executive guise and expect the total conglomeration to survive and prosper. Statistics suggest that about half of them do, but this may have more to do with the chairman's skill, tough brinkmanship bargaining and, above all, their inability to live commercially without each other. The non-executives as a body occasionally promote measures for what is termed the 'common good' – otherwise known as keeping a fragile peace.

Comment

'The best joint-venture board meetings I ever attended were in Bombay. The chairman was

> a civilised Madrassi who spoke English so fast and with such a strong accent as to be totally incomprehensible to any Englishman – but not to fellow Indians.
>
> The agendas were normally substantial volumes of about fifty pages. The meetings lasted an average of twelve minutes; millions of pounds and crates of rupees were invested and shuffled around in seconds. A loud air-conditioner behind the chairman exacerbated the complete inability to know what was going on.
>
> A gigantic Sikh, with a large dagger, stationed menacingly behind the chairman, ensured good discipline.
>
> Any vague pipings-up about why a million or so should be spent on a tawdry scheme, say, were brushed aside with "All this has been gone into very thoroughly – please refer to the relevant memorandum. Anyone else object – no, sorry you are out-voted – next please . . .". The only way to get your view over was by private lobbying a month before the meeting. Moral: carry a dagger with you at all times.'

NATIONALISED INDUSTRIES

Few in number, and getting fewer each year, nationalised industries are nevertheless ideal subjects for heavyweight non-executive contribution. They need people whose balanced views can embrace global economics and the implications on national programmes of shifts in political power and long-term strategic investment, yet still be in tune with short-term changes in customer service, labour relations and advanced technology.

About forty years ago, two key principles of appointment were agreed: the criteria of competence and ability rather than representation; and that people should be from outside the industry rather than from within. The size of the boards is surprisingly small, averaging about ten, of whom the majority are part time or non-executive. Industrialists are the most numerous, as may be expected, with bankers a respectable second. These are followed by engineers and civil servants, with trade unionists and scientists bringing up the rear.

Knighthoods, peerages and lesser honours are an obvious seal of eligibility. However, the method of selection and appointment has continued to be a subject of controversy. Until recently only 'the Departments' held lists of suitable candidates and these were watched, in true imperial fashion, by all-powerful mandarins. After due consultation in their own labyrinthine ways, a short list of recommendations was submitted to the appropriate minister who, with virtually unfettered discretion, decided which candidate appeared to be 'best for the job'. The chairman in those days enjoyed only minor powers of veto, being aware that the minister also appointed the chairman and, if given the chance, was prone to nominate the chief executive as well. It is suggested that the process is now all very different, but no one has said how.

> **Comment**
> A senior civil servant, when discussing the search brief for the replacement chairman of a government authority, said the following: 'It's all well and good your asking these exacting questions but we just do not know what the qualities, abilities and specification of the incumbent should be – at least not until we have found someone whom we intend to appoint.'

With increasing emphasis on market forces, free enterprise philosophy and privatisation, the nature, style and choice of chairmen are changing and, when they are required to sit in the highly exposed, up-front seat of responsibility, so is chairmen's willingness meekly to accept the dictates of others as to who joins the board. Even in their most euphoric moments chairmen do not expect the rules of the game to be rewritten overnight. Few, however, oppose having wider powers in selecting non-executives, making realistic levels of payment, outlawing token appointments and reversing powers of veto. The quality and ability of nationalised industry boards could only improve as a result.

What most chairmen find less comfortable to live with is the speed and frequency of ministerial changes and the knock-on effect such changes have on policy, strategy and personal relationships. Working within politically motivated constraints adds an unnecessary burden to the job. When some of these particular burdens are removed and when objectives are both clear and consistent, the boards of the massive continuing public corporations can perhaps be expected to improve their performance.

After privatisation, for example, the style, composition and balance of the boards of these same industries were transformed. Lord King and Sir John Egan have aptly demonstrated the inherent ability of people at all levels within their organisations, and the unwieldy British Telecom is now leaner and fitter in mind and body. British Rail, the electricity industry and the ten water authorities now have the chance to reinforce that point.

> **Comment**
> 'It was suggested to me that I should do two things before accepting the chairmanship of a nationalised industry. One was to become financially independent, and the other was to obtain a knighthood. I have done neither, but now fully realise the wisdom of both.'

Internationalism

In a business sense the world is getting smaller. Countries are now seen in similar proportions to the way English counties were looked upon a century ago. The City, with its global tentacles and twenty-four-hour clock, still remains United Kingdom's biggest export earner and may remain so to the embarrassment of UK primary manufacturing industries.

Further interlocking barriers to trade will disappear during the 1990s. Multinationalism is now not just an economic reality; it is an inescapable way of life for commercially interdependent nations.

It is worth emphasising that any company which plans to trade in excess of £50 million overseas should have not only an executive director with an appropriate linguistic talent but also at least one supporting foreign national on its board, as either a non-executive or an executive, probably the former. A crucial ingredient of trading with success in the global market-place, and with multinational bases, is not just an understanding of each country's people and culture but a knowledge of how each business system works in Leningrad, Frankfurt, Madrid or Tokyo. The impetus for that knowledge and understanding must begin at the top – in the boardroom.

UK companies, whose English natural tongue is the world's most used and understood language, begin with one priceless advantage, which in this century at least has not been exploited fully. Not only is the documentation of universal authorities invariably printed in English, but a basic knowledge of the language is almost obligatory for those who attend international trade, economic or political gatherings. The boards of UK companies could, with some forethought, develop a unique international flavour and style that would be the envy of other nations.

BOC is an international group based in England whose board of about twelve includes only half who are British nationals. Successive chairmen have ensured that its non-executive members possess a global perspective, are acquainted with most of the countries in which the group operates and may from time to time be used to carry out assignments abroad. BOC thinks, plans and works in an international context – its continued success is no surprise.

Companies from competitive trading nations in Europe, South America, Africa and the Far East still suffer innumerable problems caused by differences in communication and interpretation. The position in Japan was well described by Shoichi Saba, who when interviewed by George Bull said:

> The fact that Japanese is spoken at all board meetings creates a formidable language barrier. Currently, the only practical way we can use foreign executives is as advisers to the board or to the executive committees. In small circles, it is possible to speak English. As the new generation is speaking more and more English, there is a real possiblity that things might change.

Already probably the commercially best-informed nation in the world, the Japanese would have enormous added momentum if their language was as international as English. Change is already under way. The main board of Sony now includes two non-Japanese nationals. Many more are scattered among a series of joint ventures and other companies are following suit. A high proportion of Japan's rising executives have been educated, lived or worked outside their country. They are multilingual and, having studied other cultures and systems, are now returning to Japan. Their influence is clearly evident as Japan's leading corporations plan a continuing trade offensive into both the United States and a widening European market, favouring trade penetration and satellite bases as the main thrust and using mergers or acquisitions only in a support capacity.

CONCLUSION

An almost infinite variety of company sizes and situations may present a fascinating range of opportunities for the non-executive but, in itself, the appointment of a non-executive director is only paying lip service to current corporate fashion. The non-executive director's role begins to have meaning and value only when it adds strength to a board's total capability. It is likely to be fruitful only when the incoming non-executive, the chairman and existing directors share a joint commitment as to purpose, use and expected contribution. This principle of joint commitment applies whatever the size or style of company.

3

Misnomers and Mismatches

It is a Member of Parliament of exceptional modesty who does not need to suppress a simmering ambition to write an autobiography of great distinction. In a similar way, most people involved in the world of business, however remotely, have a near-irresistible urge to direct the course which others should follow. In each instance ability is not assumed to be a limiting factor – only opportunity.

Directorship, the position of being a director, is arguably the most misunderstood concept in business life today. It implies a degree of responsibility which in legal terms remains only notionally acknowledged. To an executive, a seat on the board may represent the pinnacle of achievement in the management pyramid. To a non-executive, both title and seat are still so open to loose interpretation that the role can be conveniently used to mean all things to all men – and to the occasional woman.

In order to examine the role of the non-executive, it may help first to examine the true extent of independence in today's non-executives then follow by suggesting some factors which can place the incumbent's performance in jeopardy.

INDEPENDENCE

Independence is almost universally accepted as one of the key criteria in judging the suitability of a non-executive, yet in practice it remains as elusive as a will-o'-the-wisp. It first came to prominence as a virtue in directors when the pioneering companies were formed over a century ago. Then the term, like that of 'non-executive' itself, declined in meaningful usage until the early 1980s. Prominent among the voices then clamouring for its reinstatement, almost as a permanent prefix to the non-executive director's title, was Bob Tricker who, in his book *The Independent Director*, proposed independence as an essential ingredient in non-executives, whom he also prescribed should be in the majority on audit committees. Later, in 1982, the Institute of Directors defined independence in some detail in its booklet *A Code of Practice for Non-Executive Directors*. In 1987 PRO NED followed with variations on the theme in its splendid publication *A Practical Guide for Non-Executive Directors*.

Words of wise counsel on the advantages of independence rumble on and on, largely unheeded. In a comprehensive PRO NED survey in 1989 of non-executive directors in medium and large companies, one of the questions referred to the number of main board non-executive directors who were considered to be independent. The criterion used – being without previous involvement as an employee, professional adviser, supplier or customer – was not exhaustive by any means. The average board size among the many hundreds of companies which responded was nine, and of those between three and four were non-executive. In answering, 90 per cent claimed that at least one of their non-executives was indeed independent by the above criterion. Without wishing to nit-pick, the terminology is important, for 'at least one' clearly does not mean nearly two or at least two or even between one and two. To simplify the equation a positive assumption might be that in a board size of nine directors three are certainly non-executive and of those one is certainly independent.

Accepting that, the question which immediately springs to mind is: what about the other two? In the real world of the non-executive they are to be found at boardroom tables for a multiplicity of reasons and generally fall into the following types:

- Economical 'in-house consultants'.
- A growing number of part-time executives who have a specific responsibility and spend some thirty to a hundred days a year with the company.
- Those having family or other relationships with the chairman or another director.
- Ex-executives now retired from the business.
- 'Names' or trophy directors from whom the chairman derives personal satisfaction in adding to his or her collection.
- Nominees or representatives of financial institutions, particular shareholdings or sectional interests.
- Overcommitted professionals who squeeze in an appearance or return a call but too often are unavailable.
- The early, middle or late retired who still desperately need something to do.
- Smooth-talking, well-connected easy riders who butterfly with style and grace from company to company.
- The entrenched, who came in an open-ended arrangement, are apparently there in perpetuity and will fight tooth and nail before being removed.
- People who derive personal kudos and some spin-off benefit from having their names associated with the company.
- 'Pawns' used to maintain a particular balance of power.
- Those with a very singular objective: money.

This is a brief, by no means exhaustive, and perhaps unsympathetic description of directors whose good intentions are not usually in doubt. The list is intended to illustrate two things which directors who are not independent appear to have in common:

- Collectively they represent a clear majority of the non-executives on the boards of UK companies today.
- The reason for them being there will almost surely prejudice their independence as a non-executive.

Each company, through its board and shareholder approval, is free to appoint whichever directors it may choose. If some or all of its non-executives can be described in the above terms, then that is entirely the company's affair. But if objectivity and independence are the acclaimed cornerstones of a non-executive director's value, we still have a long way to go before not 'at least one' but 'at least two' of the non-executives are considered to be fully independent.

In the meantime the role, with its exacting personal demands, is becoming more widely appreciated and those who perform it well are easier to recognise. At times, however, stylistic definitions are somewhat extravagant. In her book, *On the Edge of the Organisation: The role of the outside director* (1983) Anne Spencer refers to the occupational hazards of the role in terms akin to pathological fears, negative fantasies or existential risks – others have been less generous!

It is worth examining some of the listed points from a different angle because at the time of appointment the effect of such basic limitations may not be apparent. In considering these, three issues spring readily to mind:

- Dependence.
- Incompetence.
- Mistaken identity.

DEPENDENCE

Just as the purpose of independence has been highlighted, so the causes of its antithesis need some scrutiny, especially how dependence can subject a non-executive to the deliberations of others for nomination, appointment and continuance in the role. These are situations which appear to stem from two main sources.

One is prior executive responsibilities in the same company. In the categories of company mentioned it is probably not wildly adventurous to suggest that one ex-executive director will be found in two out of every three boardrooms, and there is no evidence to suggest that this proportion changes materially as company size decreases. It would be unfair to imply that all the stalwarts in these ex-executive legions should, for this reason alone, be discounted as ineffective. Nevertheless, with rare exceptions, they are unlikely to exercise judgement which is totally independent.

However, an impoverished performance is virtually guaranteed either when an ex-executive's experience is limited to that company, or when his or her other on-going external interests are not business oriented. An equally dismal result may be expected if the change to non-executive status is nothing more than a traditional way of easing an executive through the pangs of withdrawal from commercial life, of providing some early retirement compensation, of saving face in a forced departure or of giving a tidy remuneration perk which is classed as consultancy.

Secondly, grace-and-favour appointments are found in similar proportions, and even stronger inclinations toward dependence exist among those who are clearly beholden to someone else for their very existence. Friends of the chairman usually head the ratings, with family ties or special relationships, including power balancing and reciprocity, competing for second place. A dwindling number of non-executives first kept their seats warm a decade or more ago and are now too comfortable to move.

INCOMPETENCE

There is undoubtedly a reversal of Parkinson's law in the equation between a board's expectation of its non-executives and what they subsequently contribute. When institutions or board members urge a chairman towards non-executive recruitment and the whole process becomes a confusing embarrassment, it is not surprising if the chairman clutches at any plausible candidate suggested by a friend, professional adviser or business colleague.

Alternatively, when those who have power in the boardroom are reluctant to accept the notion of non-executives or doubt their value, they usually put together a brief which is so precise in content and time that prospective non-executive directors are left in no doubt as to their required input – and the softness of shoe they should wear. Sometimes the specifics imply constraints which will deter anyone who has in mind to play a creative role. Such limitations do not unfortunately deter the ardent position-hunters, and the level of non-executive competence falls as a result. On the other hand, a chairman familiar with the routine will concentrate his or her brief on the key issues concerning the fusion of personal chemistry among co-directors and the balance of skills and experience around the table – and will leave considerable leeway for a non-executive director to take initiatives.

This divergence of approach and expectation indicates the proportion of chairmen and co-directors who, in spite of all the promotional effort, are still not adequately acquainted with the key aspects of the non-executive function. They often do not know what to expect in the form of contribution or how to recognise the characteristics of a person who is likely to be adept in this role. So when the recruitment door is opened and a bewildering medley of availables, possibles or probables comes into view, the risks of an unskilled chairman making an unsatisfactory appointment are higher than any business would consider acceptable in a normal commercial context.

> **Comment**
> 'The growth and operating performance of a company is a direct reflection of the effectiveness and decision-making quality of its board.'

If one accepts this fundamental principle, then any inclination towards indiscriminate non-executive selection spells unnecessary risk to both board and company. The question is: can that risk be quantified and put into perspective? Not easily, but with the advantage of hindsight and some years of working on the subject a fair assessment might be as follows:

- The proportion of ready, willing and available volunteers who are likely to be competent in the non-executive role is no greater than one in every three candidates – and that is before the matching process begins.
- When haphazard methods are used to select and match a non-executive director to a company's needs, the probability of making a successful appointment is about 10 per cent.
- A chairman, even though not fully acquainted with either the non-executive role or the selection process, can notably improve those odds by sheer application to the task – perhaps to a figure of 40 per cent.
- Chairmen who are comfortable and well versed in the process, and have professional guidance or use search, achieve quite different results. Their expectation of success is high – about 75 per cent, or three to one in favour.

The embarrassment of recruiting either a misnomer or a mismatch clearly demonstrates the value of a chairman who has an aptitude for this aspect of the job. No one prescribes the haphazard route, but it is one frequently followed for want of guidance – and there is a world of risk difference between the odds of ten to one against and three to one in favour. This range of likely results is not just theory; it is reflected by disappointing non-executive performance in countless boardrooms up and down the country.

Non-executives are expected to be knowledgeable and experienced in most if not all board matters. Yet these abilities have to be acquired. To suggest, as some do, that such abilities are the automatic product of board experience as an executive is about as naïve as claiming that one achieves a low handicap at golf simply by walking the course! It is unreasonable to assume that a non-executive title, once given, endows the holder with timeless and universal aptitude in that role.

Comment

'Beware the non-executive who is looking for an appointment for purposes of prestige.'

MISTAKEN IDENTITY

Some chairmen, especially those in smaller companies, are attracted to the view that recruiting a workable non-executive director is an economical alternative to using a consultant. At first sight the assumption may seem to be justified. After all, a fair proportion of people are prepared to carry out short- or long-term assignments and probably already do so either to make up a planned portfolio of interests or to provide essential revenue.

Generally, however, these plans fail to live up to their initial expectations either because the solo specialist runs out of steam or because the so-called non-executive director's independent and objective thrust diminishes as his or her role changes markedly from board colleague to client's contractual adviser. It is ill-judged to confuse the consultant's role with that of the non-executive, or to go for a 'buy one, get one free' bargain deal. In recent years the term 'consultant' has been so misused that its original professional status has all but disappeared, forcing the consulting organisations, which provide an immense range of services, to drop the term 'consultant' in favour of identification by name.

Comment

One day, a lawyer telephoned to find out the level of non-executive director fees he should ask a client who had invited him to join his board. To the question 'How much total time will you be devoting to that role, including homework and travel?' his response was 'Three or four hours a month, and I plan to charge by the hour'. In a few moments we established a most forgetful relationship. Perhaps his client was well pleased with whatever bargain was struck, but it had nothing to do with a non-executive role.

Similar problems of identity happen when the non-executive role is combined with that of the part-time executive, even though their descriptive titles indicate a fairly clear contradiction in terms. There is no reason why an executive who works on a regular part-time basis should not be invited to join a board, but everyone should understand that the independent non-executive element does not feature in such an appointment. There is, in fact, every reason to promote the use of part-time executives (see Chapter 10).

CONCLUSION

Helping to run a company in any capacity is important but the question of a board appointment must be kept separate, for in that role the quality of a non-executive director has to stand on its own merit.

4

The Non-Executive Profile

It was the late Sir Maurice Dean, one of the doyens amongst promoters of the non-executive director cause, who said: 'Nowadays it takes more than a name to do the non-executive job as boardroom responsibilities and the way they are discharged come under increased scrutiny.' He expressed this view almost twenty years ago, yet the debate still continues as to exactly what characteristics should be embraced within the word 'more'.

It is all too easy to fall into the trap of listing a series of esoteric qualities which no single being could possibly have, and then to claim the virtually unlimited curative powers of the possessors. No two non-executive roles are the same; each has to relate to the culture, type, size, composition and circumstance of the company board to which an appointment is made. The needs of a vibrant small private business in no way equate with those of a nationalised industry, and a non-executive director with interest and enthusiasm to join one would feel less than comfortable about effectively serving the other. Even in companies of similar size the input required from their non-executives is surprisingly variable.

Comment
'When first I was appointed I was very clear as to my legal and moral responsibilities, but all the research one can do – reading background material, attending seminars – does not prepare one for the real world

> which each different company represents. Now several directorships later I know the multiplicity of contributions which were needed. They included being involved in takeovers, marketing, public relations, recruitment and defence contracts, quite apart from showing both independence and a strong shoulder when appropriate.'

MOTIVATIONS

On the face of it no one in their right mind should willingly agree to lock themselves into a commitment which at times is burdensome, never boasts of high financial rewards and occasionally may present risks of personal legal liability. But non-executives do so, and in increasing numbers. Why?

Prestige

Prestige can scarcely be a consideration because a non-executive director worth having usually comes from an organisation or activity of at least comparable size, responsibility and complexity. Having one's name on the letter heading has now lost much of its appeal and is almost unfashionable. 'It takes more than a name' is more than just a comment; it is a widely shared belief.

Money

Until recently, fees paid to non-executive directors were almost a joke. Even now, post-tax incremental income, to someone already active in other fields, is modest by any standards and especially when the cumulative time, effort and responsibility are taken into account. Fees are frequently paid to the non-executive's mainstream company and no direct monetary benefits result.

It becomes a different picture if there is a 'professional' intention in acquiring a portfolio of directorships as a means of livelihood. Apart from having other undesirable aspects, such monetary bondage sorely tests the exercise of independence. In another dimension, a non-executive director's attitude and perspective can be severely distorted by the leverage of money, a situation often apparent when a seat on the board is taken primarily to look after a personal or family stake in the business. If a non-executive acts for money he is less likely to disagree with the person who signs the cheque. When representing a personal, family or company stake, priority is often assessed by judging what is in the best interests of that stakeholder – and at that time. However, this may not also represent the best interests of either the company or the remaining shareholders – especially in hostile bids and buy-outs.

Co-directors have a right to expect each of their non-executive directors already to have successful careers and to have proved their worth in the outside world. One important representation of that achievement is financial autonomy.

Keeping occupied

Non-executive roles are a major attraction for those who have retired and who wish to retain a link with business in order to keep their minds active and to offer wise counsel in return. Sadly, once retired, people rapidly become distanced from the everyday business world and find that disappointment and frustration usually accompany this route. When the only alternative is gardening it is already too late to think of picking up the non-executive director's baton.

Affinity

Without being close enough to risk a conflict of interests, non-executive directors are frequently attracted to, or sought by, a company where the nature of its business is one in which they have a natural affinity and feel at ease. They can assimilate key elements without a protracted learning curve and are quickly in tune with scale, terminology and pace of change.

Affinity should not be confused with expertise, and unless one of the reasons for being appointed is to strengthen a board's knowledge in a specific discipline non-executive directors are not expected to be experts in either the technical aspects of a company's business or its operational methods. However, being a director, the non-executive should from time to time visit operating plants and offices or join in management workshops and must be generally well informed. Without some natural affinity backed by a fair measure of homework, a non-executive director runs the risk of visibly floundering while trying to interpret the words and pictures, instead of understanding the messages they convey.

Relationships

When people get together with an enterprise in mind, expectations are seldom realised unless the group produces a volition greater than the sum of its parts. Bonds which are found more often among the executive team than in the boardroom usually reflect a chief executive's ability to take the lead in creating a buoyant spirit within top management. The chief executive knows that the team must have attitudes which can override the obstacles found in everyday operating life. Leadership in developing relationships has little to do with either family or self-interest.

In contrast, uncomfortable, less-experienced chairmen tend to run their board meetings along a carefully timed agenda and with such civilised formality that they all but stifle the natural instincts for creativity and enterprise among its members. While they are absolutely right to emphasise that meetings of the board are distinct from those of executive management in content, purpose and the attendance of outside directors, no excuses can vindicate chairmen who preside over a soggy, spiritless assembly. Even if they flourish in such a climate, their boards seldom do.

The armoury of a discriminating non-executive director should include the resource to deduce quietly both a chairman's style and the resulting boardroom ambience – and to do it before making a commitment. If at any stage the indications are sinister, prudence suggests a diplomatic withdrawal from the scene unless the non-executive believes his or her role is to help change the very fabric of the board. Joining with co-directors in a stimulating endeavour is one of the real joys of the job; being instrumental in bringing about fundamental change in the boardroom may be another, but it is suicidal for a non-executive to misread indications of the state of internal board relationships.

It is equally disastrous for non-executive directors to develop relationships with any co-director which may prejudice their ability to contribute even-handedly to the board and show that special quality of loyal independence towards all its members. Confrontation between executives is commonplace and seldom gets out of hand, but when a chief executive and his chairman have antlers locked in combat, firm and fast intervention by the non-executives is imperative. If a special relationship is perceived, the warring factions only intensify the hostilities and hope of regaining accord is usually lost.

Broadening experience

Adding another dimension to one's business career is as attractive and satisfying as in any other sphere of interest, and taking a non-executive role is doing exactly that.

A board invitation is of almost irresistible appeal. It is less easy subsequently to work outside one's familiar structure, to apply the self-discipline required to acquit oneself among colleagues of contrasting style, to adapt to an unrelated business, to accept the attributable risks and to do it with enthusiasm for comparative peanuts. Those who can perform really do contribute and also add another dimension to their own experience. And since it is experience in the 'real world', it can be favourably compared with working through ten case studies at Harvard or a similar business school. Chairmen increasingly welcome approaches being made to their executives from non-competitive companies.

Opportunity to contribute

Making a contribution is the ultimate in satisfaction for a non-executive director – or at least for one who has something to offer. Nothing motivates better than a clear brief of the tasks which lie ahead and the promise of more to come. Nothing kills interest and enthusiasm faster than a chairman waffling through a series of platitudes or ill-considered responses when asked the simple question: what do you expect of me?

The absence of knowledge and understanding of the non-executive role frequently limits the ability of both chairman and co-directors to explore fully the scope and expected contribution from a new addition to the board. When 'interviewing' a prospective colleague, those who are unfamiliar with the role try to avoid expressions of positive opinion and keep the discussion in a state of inconsequential generalities – except perhaps to check whether chemistry is positive and the 'candidate' adequately house trained!

Such shortcomings result in fitting square pegs into round holes. They frustrate efforts to create an effective board and deter people who are otherwise willing and able to be of value.

QUALITIES AND PROFILES

Conventional wisdom today portrays the non-executive as a fairly bland, pear-shaped individual, full of admirable qualities and few surprises. As this book aims to expand knowledge rather than issue edicts, it may be fruitful to explore these attributes from less conventional directions.

Qualities are considered here neither in order of importance nor with the thought that their possession automatically creates a 'Super-NED'. They do not pre-empt the need correctly to match individual to company, but when added in fair measure to suitable personality and relationships, they make for a non-executive of presence and character.

Awareness

Sir Kenneth Cork has written: (*Code of Practice for the Non-Executive Director,* IoD, 1982): 'In my professional experience, I have come across many companies which have fallen into difficult times, only to find that their non-executive directors were conspicuous by their absence from the problems of the company.' Such absences may be unintentional, but non-executive directors have a duty to watch the function of the board and to propose through the chairman any changes which seem necessary. To do this a non-executive has to be aware of events and take stock of what is really going on in and around the boardroom – irrational prejudices, power cliques, questionable decisions and subsequent implications.

To be fully aware, a non-executive should be able to interpret the body language of colleagues. Changes in posture, an involuntary nod or head movement, the grunt of pent-up frustration, an eyelid's flicker to convey success to another, the quick gathering of breadth and resources – all these are indications of critical moments being experienced by co-directors under pressure and each discloses a wealth of unintentional information.

Not to know or to conveniently turn a blind eye negates the function of the non-executive director. Unlike executives, a non-executive director has only one *raison d'être* – to contribute towards improving board performance – and that demands awareness.

Ability to communicate

The power to express opinions and persuade others is an elusive and highly prized asset which, although as dependent on adeptness in timing as on the use of words, also brings into play personal presence, credibility, innate determination and the prudent use of leverage. Between co-directors such powers are probably exercised more outside than inside the boardroom.

Oddly enough the best way for a non-executive director to communicate is usually to begin by listening, a prerequisite to being either a useful sounding board or an adviser. Then, when the time comes to talk, no matter what the occasion or absence of advanced warning, a non-executive is expected to respond with clarity and in short, simple and human terms.

These skills are far from easy to acquire let alone to put into action, but they remain one of the criteria by which a non-executive's performance is judged. While driving or shuttling back home after a meeting, it is useless to think over what one might have said, or how a point could have been made with wit and panache – the moment has gone, it is already too late. In communicating, non-executive directors have no tomorrows.

Integrity

Integrity is a quality that hardly needs mentioning. Everyone wants it but many fail the test when their time comes. To err is human, but it is not acceptable for non-executives. True personal and financial independence, and the absence of any conflicting relationships past or present, add credence but not guarantees – and with non-executive directors there are no guarantors!

Risks, which are normally low, loom larger when predators are sniffing or a stakeout is being made as a prelude to buying control cheaply through the side door. Non-executives are obvious sources of information and may be identified as targets to be courted into compromising situations or encouraged to make imprudent disclosures.

The legal system now takes a harsh view of such insider complacency or trading – if and when it can be proven, long after the event. In the immediate term it remains a matter of vigilance to be properly exercised by the chairman.

Judgement

There is no place in the boardroom for non-executive directors who are short on judgemental quality. The respect of every colleague and the quality of every decision will depend upon it, and getting it right includes the 'when and how': when to speak or act, and how to do it effectively.

Some companies prosper under the wisdom of a single Solomon, or in adversity have a trouble-shooting chief executive or 'white knight' chairman thrust upon them to mastermind recovery. A single dominant force can work well for a time provided a balancing caucus of independence exists in the non-executives. Without such balance, excessive power in one seat will diminish a board's creative ability. Dictators avoid exposing chinks in their armour and are prone to look outside for advice and thought-provoking stimulatives, a process which excludes co-directors and destroys confidence between board members.

In exercising judgement a board normally expects its non-executives to apply their individual and combined talents to help make a thorough scrutiny of executive proposals and to minimise the margin of error when decisions are finally taken. On these occasions, executives look for competence in their non-executives – just as later, when decisions are put to the test and carried out, the non-executives will expect from them a reciprocal standard of performance.

There is strong support for the opinion that inputs of vision are the critical catalysts in the process of fine tuning a board's judgemental ability. Without being able to relate to some future objective, policy and strategic deliberations among directors tend to be sterile. In smaller companies an owner/manager is often guided by one of the non-executives, whose task it is both to initiate and to develop a practical vision of the future. In larger organisations the chief executive and chairman, acting as a dynamic duo, are invariably the focus of such a vision.

However, in guiding a board in its judgemental function a chairman has a unique input to make. Only the chairman can:

- Create a climate in which thought and expression may flourish naturally.
- Bring both individual and collective views together in a cohesive form.
- Ensure awareness of what has been decided.

A non-executive director, while avoiding the danger of usurping the chairman, needs to observe and make yet another judgement. He or she must be satisfied that the board, being the centre of a company's accumulated perceptions, builds upon this supply of information through discussions which stretch the minds of directors and produce astute decisions – provided, of course, that the board is not subject to the will of a so-called 'benevolent' dictator which deprives it of the ability to think at all.

Judgements, like board decisions, are seldom flashes of inspiration born around the table. Most grow into their final shape during analytical build-up and debate among executive directors and they are rarely transformed significantly on sanction day, the quality of judgement remaining both elusive and intangible until viewed with hindsight.

Creativity

The once predominant policing or watchdog role of the non-executive director is rapidly disappearing. Non-executives, while still mindful of due caution, now favour creative involvement in policy and strategic issues and face-to-face discussion with executives to learn more about, or to question, their opinions and the reasoning behind them. To do this, non-executives themselves need to be positive. It is no longer acceptable for a non-executive to act as a self-appointed obstacle to be scaled before almost any board decision is made.

Comment
A chairman related his experience of an erroneous non-executive appointment in this way: 'During the first six months he said very little. In the next his comments failed to invite attention. Now he damn well says no to everything – I suspect in order to let us know he is there.'

An equally woeful example was concisely summed up by a colleague with the phrase: 'He is someone who says expecting the worst is being too optimistic.'

Humour

A humourless board contains few escape valves for the tensions which are bound to arise from time to time. Meetings are generally perceived to be formal, serious and rather dull occasions – 'dignified' was a term frequently used to obscure a myriad of personal agonies.

An unspoken but guiding maxim of directors in many companies is: wit is the exclusive province of the boss – and let no one dare forget it. Even in these instances there is usually a natural butt or whimsical joker around the table on whom the boss can feed. If not, board life can consist of endless variations on the theme of 'Fred, when I want your opinion, I'll give it to you'!

Perhaps surprisingly, the majority of boardrooms do enjoy a sense of fun which bubbles away beneath the surface, frequently erupting almost unconsciously amid occasions of both celebration and crisis. The repartee is often quick and incisive, containing more than a suggestion of personal rivalry and prowess.

Within the armoury of the new non-executive director should lie the talent to add a touch of humour here, defuse an explosive situation there and help quell the apprehensions which may inhibit others. A non-executive can liberate the notion not only that humour is a natural companion in the boardroom, but that its absence rapidly induces a dreary state of mental sterility.

Courage to act

Many have witnessed acts of considerable nerve in the expression of personal convictions during either formal or informal meetings of the board. This is especially so when the need arises to initiate fundamental change, settle differences between combative forces or resolve critical policy issues.

Within the cosiness of collective responsibility, when the crunch of decision time arrives it can be easier and less painful to go along with the mood or particular persuasion of the day. It requires little effort to remain silent and let others risk their heads on the block or to watch a potentially damaging course of action be chosen yet fail to protest or offer words of warning. Silence does not mean consent, but I have yet to meet anyone who does not admit that at some time they too have lacked the courage to speak.

A weakness or omission of this nature in the character of non-executive directors destroys the very reason for their existence let alone their own confidence. A non-executive's credibility demands quite the opposite, even to the extent of stopping a meeting in its tracks if necessary. Those who bend in the breeze should recognise their own basic flaw, decline the role and so avoid the turbulence to which, sooner or later, every non-executive is exposed.

Although it is not common, non-executive directors can and do act in concert to bring about either major policy changes or the removal of a chairman, a chief executive or both. These are not actions which are taken lightly and it requires courage, determination and personal risk to see them through when the soft option is to walk away. This seldom-publicised form of non-executive intervention does occur more frequently than is generally imagined. A notable example was Lord Keith, never a man to shirk a challenge, who in the mid 1980s led his non-executive colleagues in ousting the chairman of STC and within twelve months repeated the exercise at Beechams. In the latter organisation he had been involved in a similar boardroom coup about thirty years earlier. One has to wonder whether any non-executive director's term of office should allow them to be there for a second time without them having noticed the problem building up, and having taken the necessary action to avoid such an ousting.

Independence

In the past decade there has been a growing lobby in favour of prefixing the non-executive director title with the word 'independent', for there is no more important attribute for the title-holder to possess.

The Institute of Directors has long recommended that, regardless of the number of directors who use the title 'non-executive', a company should have at least two who are genuinely independent. This view is reinforced by the Stock Exchange which now requires non-executive representation on the boards of all companies seeking a full or USM listing. However, interpretation of the concept of independence is still conveniently loose and open to abuse.

A definition of independence which I commend to you is: not having any contractual or other relationship with the company or its directors apart from the current office of director and not being subject to any control or influence of a third party which could affect the exercise of independent judgement. It is, of course, understood that a company may also choose to appoint others who are not independent because their relationship may stem from prior executive responsibility, association with the company's professional advisers, or representation of financial institutions, major shareholders or various sectional interests.

These views have been endorsed and upheld on countless occasions and they remain the bedrock of accepted wisdom on the subject. Some consider that such a definition of independence is too stringent or suggest that it may imply less than total virtue on the part of those excluded by its exacting terms. In response, it is arguable that even today the potential benefits attached to independence are not well enough appreciated, let alone activated. It is not a question of assessing the soundness or otherwise of intentions; other factors being equal, non-executives who are known and perceived to be independent begin with a distinct advantage. They are not beholden, they are not dependent on financial rewards and their free expression of opinion is subject to neither leverage nor prejudice.

In the European two-tier system, supervisory board members are all non-executive under a part-time chairman who also acts as a link with the executive board. The non-executives are not all independent and it would be hard for employee directors or representatives of financial interests to claim otherwise. In Holland the employee and shareholder representatives jointly appoint an independent 'blocking third'. In Germany there can be a straight fifty-fifty representation of employees and shareholders, without a specified requirement for independents; in practice, however, they are invariably included.

ASSESSING RELATIVE QUALITIES

A question often raised is how a relative value might be assigned to all the intrinsic qualities frequently considered in connection with today's non-executive. There is no set formula and it seems sensible that this should remain a matter of individual perception and judgement. However, the following suggestions may provide a starting point for those interested in making their own assessments. Using a 0 to 10 rating scale the top twenty might be as shown in Figure 4.1. Probably the only forced choice is integrity, since without that everything becomes suspect.

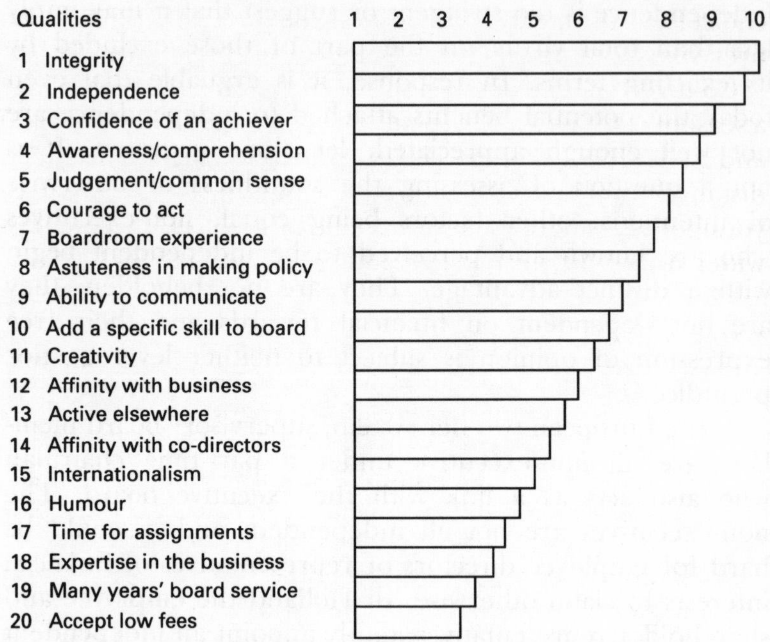

Figure 4.1 Qualities of the non-executive director

Before delving into other aspects of the non-executive profile, however blurred they may be, a quotation attributed to Felix Cohen comes to mind: 'Generally, the theories we believe we call facts and the facts we disbelieve we call theories.' Aiming to strike a balance between theory and fact might be a rational way to progress this book's objective of expanding knowledge on the subject.

Age

Non-executive directors are generally within the age-range of forty to sixty at the time of appointment. There are, of course, highly effective non-executives who are older, some by a considerable margin, but they are either already into their term of office or splendid exceptions to the rule. Given choice, a chairman looks for a non-executive who is not much over sixty, and anticipates a three- to six-year stint.

Co-directors welcome a non-executive director who brings a seasoned approach to problems yet is youthful in both mind and style. The side-effects of enforced early retirement, distance from the business scene and a wide age-gap with younger executives are just three factors which weigh against wider use of people in their middle or late sixties.

> **Comment**
> A chief executive commented on his experience in a unitary board with five – a majority – of non-executive directors: 'The management of the company was left entirely in the hands of the executive, and was demonstrably successful. The function of the non-executives, who were all very active executives in their own businesses, was to promote and support, to hire and fire senior officers and to take over specific tasks or emergencies that clearly the executives could not handle. One feature of the non-executives was that, with the exception of one, they were all under fifty'. He reflected further by adding: 'The message to me seems clear in that, provided they are young, active, professional businessmen who do not involve themselves in the running of the company, the non-executives can play a valuable part.'

Present downward age trends are likely to continue, although greater use of non-executive directors coupled with the introduction of more two-tier concepts should sustain demand over quality of supply.

Years alone are not the crux of a non-executive's contribution, since some people are emasculated at an early age. What matters is the character and ability of the person whose form is fired by those years. At a point in their development some people become organised, disciplined, independent in mind and attitudes, are able to balance experience with astuteness, knowledge with judgement, unbiased perceptions with skills to communicate – then a non-executive of substance is in the making. As Bernard Baruch said: 'Old age is fifteen years older than I am.'

Gender

Non-executive directors are predominantly men, to the extent of about 95 per cent. The reason lies in a similar ratio being currently found in UK boardrooms, from where most non-executives come. The very nature of the role makes it difficult to compare performance let alone to complicate the issue by a theoretical pitching of woman against man, and there is every reason why one should avoid the temptation to do so.

Of one thing there is no doubt: as the proportion of women directors continues to increase and women take wider responsibilities in executive management and in academic, senior business and professional appointments, this will be reflected in at least an equivalent rate of growth in their use as non-executives. Already the long-sustained bias towards male domination on corporate boards is decreasing, and few chairmen now decline the opportunity to have exploratory talks with prospective non-executives of either gender except on the basis of suitability.

Current status

If you want something done give it to someone who is busy. By the same principle, a non-executive should be active and involved. Any suggestion of being inactive or retired, whether forcibly or voluntarily, needs powerful compensation. This favoured busy aspect is reflected in a continuous demand for current chief executives or managing directors and executives in finance, marketing or manufacturing.

Only about one in four UK directors has a professional qualification and a minuscule proportion are involved in an advanced technology. Either attribute is a positive bonus in helping to create a well-rounded board.

In a similar way, another dimension is added to a board's cumulative knowledge when a non-executive joins who has a broader international background. Early career graduates from INSEAD in France or IMEDE in Switzerland are particularly highly sought after. Usually multilingual, they have through the years climbed the management ladder by running businesses within major groups which have global activities.

Increasingly, non-executive seats are filled by part-time chairmen of unrelated companies or seasoned businessmen and women who are committed to a multi-role career. They prove to be excellent contributors especially when their varied company experience includes City or specific international exposure. A balanced portfolio of interests is important and should include one anchor appointment involving upwards of fifty days a year.

Fewer in number but not in importance are academics, specialists, members of professional bodies and those with military or governmental careers. However, there is a danger that, at board level, their talents may be underutilised unless the group has either complex activities or is large enough to use both their individual input and their external connections. When combined with two or three other non-executive directors, perhaps from sources previously mentioned, they give a significant and stimulating lift to the whole board, especially in the development of original concepts, policy and strategic issues. They must, of course, be able to relate to the company's commercial and industrial environment.

Government connection

The influence of national and European government on business and commercial life is immense. In spite of privatisation, government influence will increase rather than decrease as a result of wider legislation both at home and from the EC. For example, European Commission proposals to outlaw insider dealing are far tougher than any which currently exist in the Community countries, including the United Kingdom. Companies whose futures are subjected to these forces, or who may be caught up in the foreseeable battles of conformity versus sovereign rights, must strengthen their boards' knowledge in this respect.

Government, for its part, is making co-operative gestures both by the secondment of civil servants into companies and by almost welcoming private-sector 'colonels' into their own ranks. The inclusion of a non-executive drawn from government or the civil service can only add to a board's awareness and understanding – provided the input can be put to good use. Cynics may suggest that it is either people with current inside information or friendly contacts who are really sought, but this is a barb which is long outdated. It is high time that the outdated separatist notions that have long restricted fruitful interaction between government, commerce and industry were cast aside. Then perhaps civil servants will be able to enrich more boardrooms with their character, wit, first-class brains and wealth of knowledge.

Comment

'In this instance the non-executives on the board, of which there were six to the five executives, were specifically chosen because of their particular expertise and background: . . . in banking, . . . in management and . . . for political experience are examples. This was an eminently successful arrangement where government interest ensured the best possible working of the board and the skills and background of the executive and non-executive directors were an invaluable mix in a very exacting management task.

Life expectancy

In all well-structured stories there is a beginning, a middle and an end. Non-executives, on the other hand, for very human reasons, are prone to favour their own particular tale continuing through a timeless middle ground of growing familiarity and contentment. Utopia is the unique seat of a spectator who sees a changing scene unfold around him without being caught up in its gyrations. It may be that the non-executive plays a valuable catalytic role for a number of years, but eventually the pointer stops and its direction becomes both threatening and unavoidable.

As well as changes resulting from resignations after mergers, acquisitions or clashes of personality, opinion and policy, a board is quite a natural evolutionary human entity. A company may be immortal, but no so its directors. Non-executives can be likened to fuel in a rocket – and are so consumed. Without fixing hard and fast parameters, a proper span for a competent non-executive director is between three and six years. Within that period nearly all the fuel of experience, knowledge and skills available to the board should have been effectively burnt up. Subsequently, the rate of replenishment is weakened by association and shows a diminishing return.

Even when a time span is openly discussed, the moment of departure is never easy to accept and on the face of it is sometimes difficult to justify. After all, why should Jim be a valued board member in March and quite dispensable in April? Another month or two obviously makes no difference, but unless time disciplines are agreed, months soon turn into years.

The principle of a planned contribution cycle is irrefutable. It is the job of the chairman to run the board and to review performance and initiate changes which keep it in shape to meet the tasks of tomorrow. Discussion of these plans will usually be held with the chief executive and non-executives. Even when contention exists, non-executives must respond positively. Their duty is to maintain the board's standing, and if asked to go they should do so with good grace, neither kowtowing nor being obstructive, and avoiding petty recriminations or false pretences. There will always be something more that could have been said, but non-executives should go with as much enthusiasm as they arrived. Both company and non-executive seem to benefit from their shared experience – and there is a life hereafter.

5

Non-Executives and the Chairman

The chairman runs the board and in that capacity is the person who has the greatest single influence on each non-executive's appointment, function and subsequent day of departure. Ironically, it is frequently also the case that the non-executives are the people who are called upon to advise or perhaps demand that the chairman recognise when the time has come for him or her to go – and then adjudicate upon a successor.

With relationships so entwined, a non-executive must fully understand not just the chairman's character and style but also the particular set of tasks that the chairman has been asked to carry out – assuming, of course, that a competent performance is expected and that the chairman is not there simply as a convenient puppet.

SCOPE OF RESPONSIBILITIES

A company's size, complexity and structure will largely dictate the calibre of the chairman and also the amount of time required for the fulfilment of duties. The chairman of a small proprietorial company, for example, may devote no more than a total of four or five days a year to that specific task, dealing on a local basis with auditors, accountants, annual returns, co-owners and the bank, and, if other directors exist, presiding over two or three short, almost obligatory meetings. The remaining time is invariably spent at the sharp end, running the day-to-day business and responding to the title 'boss' in preference to either 'chairman' or 'managing director'.

By contrast, in a major international group the span of its chairman's contribution will be immense. Quite apart from an exacting board, shareholder and City programme, the chairman's role will be likely to include involvement in mergers and acquisitions, representation within industry, and government and overseas trade missions. The board will probably monitor both the structure and co-ordination of subsidiaries or joint ventures worldwide and relate their activities to regional changes in either economic or political balances of power. The chairman will also be the arbiter for standards of integrity and credibility within the group and ensure that it takes adequate account of such factors as health, safety, the environment and society, at policy and strategic level. The chairman's operational interface will normally be confined to a full appreciation of the chief executive's actions. This presents an imposing array of tasks, not surprisingly adding up to something approaching full time. In fact a considerable number of major group chairmen have the capacity also to act as either a part-time chairman or a non-executive director in other smaller organisations.

Within these two extremes almost any formula can be created for the scope of the chairman's responsibilities. Few of them demand an every day, every week presence unless a chairman is to some extent running one of the company's business functions or is in fact a chief executive who has chosen also to take the chair. Both are moves which significantly shift the ground on which the non-executives stand. Generally speaking, as a company grows so do the duties and responsibilities of its chairman.

TIME SPANS

Leaving aside proprietorial businesses, smaller private companies need a chairman for the equivalent of twenty to thirty days spread over a year. Once again the role of chairman is frequently dovetailed with that of chief executive, or in family businesses is taken by a senior member in addition perhaps to an executive role.

However, when a company changes to quoted status a new dimension is added to the role in the form of regular dialogue and relationship building with City institutions, stockbrokers, merchant banks and financial and public relations advisers. In the excitement of an approaching 'market day', these added commitments are seldom taken into account, although they easily increase by half the time demanded of a chairman, raising it to between thirty and fifty days. Unless the introduction of a part-time chairman has been made well ahead of going to market, these new pressures are likely to result in an already hard pressed chairman/chief executive becoming severely side-tracked from the operational function at a time when external investors are intensifying their attention on current and forecast company performance.

In medium and large companies, where the chairman will have absorbed the initial market impact, priorities turn towards making the increased equity work to enhance growth. Combining organic development with agreed acquisitions is a popular strategy and, although the chief executive may play the major role, a chairman's availability and input is vital. Hostile or complex bids can tie a chairman down for weeks at a time, and in the wake of most mergers and acquisitions time-consuming work on consolidation, restructuring and divestments is sure to follow. The ratchet again moves up a few notches and the time required now heads towards eighty or ninety days.

The major corporations could command up to 180 days but seldom do. Graham Day is a typical example of a chairman with more than one commitment. He took the chair at both Cadbury Schweppes and Rover, mixing chocolates with cars, each on a part-time basis. As overkill, or for good measure, he also prefixes his title with 'executive'.

USE OF NON-EXECUTIVE DIRECTORS

If the chairman has paid attention to creating a board with suitable composition and balance, a number of non-executives will have been included who can help both the chairman and the executives to anticipate problem areas and steer a comparatively trouble-free course. Non-executives not only have to fulfil the needs of a company by contributing directly to the board, but they must also be capable of talking frankly to the chairman about the board's performance and the chairman's own, and if necessary suggesting how they may be improved. Such comments may concern anything from minutes of meetings to fundamental changes in board membership. In most instances a close and productive relationship is formed between the chairman and the non-executives. It usually stems from arm's-length mutual respect, fostered by easy dialogue, positive chemistry and common intent.

Comment
Experienced chairmen repeat to me over and over again that the appointment of non-executive directors has been the turning point in the successful development of their companies. This has been especially so around the time of expanding into the public arena from the less demanding – in terms of boardroom activity and accountability – private company situation.

The omens for the effective use of non-executive directors are good when they are well briefed (see Chapter 13), are exposed to the operational climate and can talk freely to their chairman about company strengths or weaknesses in policy, strategy, business plans and performance. The context of such informal discussions should have a clear focus on present or future company needs and should avoid 'inner cabinet' innuendoes which may appear to exclude the chief executive or executive directors.

Comment
'Without a capable chairman, no amount of non-executive directors, no matter how excellent, can bring full benefit to a company. The chairman is the vital link between non-executives and company.'

Whether or not one feels the term 'conventional wisdom' is applicable, there is certainly no shortage of opinion voiced by non-executives as to the influence a chairman has on their own contribution, as these further remarks indicate.

Comment
'The effectiveness of non-executive directors depends largely on the way the chairman runs his board and on his willingness and ability to obtain the right contributions from them.

If he wants help in strategic direction, independent perspectives and detached views, a useful sounding board, etc., he must set out to create the right environment and opportunities for them to contribute in this way. Prospective non-executives should therefore agree in advance with the chairman how he intends the board to benefit from their appointment.'

Although in two-tier systems the chairman of the upper-tier supervisory or policy board acts as a communications link between it and the counterbalancing executive board, the chairman does not have either a dominant influence over non-executive appointments to the former or any significant weight in deciding who should serve on the latter where, of course, the chief executive occupies the chair. The converse applies in a unitary board where chairmen have the power largely to determine choice of non-executive directors, the parameters of their role and how, within or outside the boardroom, they interact with executives and senior management.

In running the board, a chairman either can exert a dominant or co-ordinating role, or, by default, forfeit the power to influence the appointment of an adequate complement of non-executives. An embattled chairman may no longer be the boardroom 'boss' and may have lost control to a faction within the board. When this happens and policies better suited to personal than company interests are being driven through, it is too late for a chairman to wish for a body of independent non-executives to correct the imbalance. The honour of taking the chair begins to have a hollow ring.

THE CHAIRMAN: A BOARDROOM ENIGMA

Ask any group of chairmen which is the most difficult aspect of their role and the majority will say, 'Handling the chief executive.' Is it any wonder then that so many choose, agree to, or devise a plausible alternative? In examining this primary board role, it may be useful to comment upon some of its time-honoured variations.

Executive chairman

This is a title which clearly states that in addition to taking the chair there exists an executive co-ordinating function. It usually indicates that a company has three or more managing directors, each reporting to the chairman, who also has the final word on action plans and decisions. The structure is frequently found in multinationals, where the position of executive chairman is a full-time seat. If the incumbent then appoints a separate chief executive to whom managing directors report, confusion is bound to follow.

Chairman and chief executive

This is an alternative and popular power base. Most proprietorial or small private companies have not reached either the stage or the size when a split in roles is feasible. Among medium and large UK companies about 40 per cent use this extremely simple solo configuration. In semi-autonomous UK subsidiaries of major US or European corporations, the percentage increases sharply, perhaps reflecting the reality that the company in fact, though not in law, has no more than divisional status.

> **Comment**
> 'Combining the chairman and chief executive roles is often the first step towards creating an unbalanced board.'

For years there has been a strong lobby against removing a crucial boardroom counterbalance by allowing one person to have this dual, often burdensome responsibility. Apart from the oversubscribed Guinness débâcle, a case in point was Rudolph Agnew who, towards the end of ConsGold's fight to stave off Minorco's bid, stated his intention to split his dual role and appoint a chief executive if they won their fight for independence. ConsGold enjoyed victory in that battle, but before Agnew had time even to regain his breath, let alone split the role, Hanson came upon the scene to win game, set and match with the precision and timing of a Wimbledon champion.

The financial dailies abound with features describing the latest addition to the ever-lengthening list of companies where rocketing good fortune has suddenly turned to disaster, either because the weight of responsibility grew too exacting for one head or the incumbent was possessed of an obsessional reluctance to share either burden or power. Yet the practice of combining the chairman and chief executive roles persists, despite pressures from the Bank of England, the City and numerous professional institutions. Chief executives continue to keep a watchful eye on the opportunity for total control, and it is they, not chairmen, who are the predominant source of initiatives to combine the roles.

Frankly it is not surprising. The chairman's role in the United Kingdom has for too long remained a sacred cow. In Japan when an ex-ambassador is made an adviser to a prestigious corporation, as many are, the process is called 'a descent from heaven'. In the United Kingdom, when a chairman is appointed, it is too often considered to be an ascent *to* heaven, as all the divine qualities associated with the position are assumed to be automatically endowed with the title.

Many chief executives now apply quite a disarming criterion when assessing the chairman's role: will the incumbent be as skilful in the performance of that job as the board may reasonably expect me to be in mine, and will the examination of credentials be carried out with equal rigour? With the comfort of having a strong case, and knowing the chances of finding a suitable chairman to be weak, chief executives may go for the devil they know, namely themselves, set their own terms and opt for duality. The task of directing the executive and running the company is demanding enough without having to keep in tune with a chairman who goes through the motions without knowing either their meaning or their purpose. It is easier and arguably more effective to do both oneself.

> **Comment**
> 'During the past four years I have had the opportunity to work with many scores of chairmen who run the boards of companies both large and small. The conclusions I draw upon their competence are disappointing and disturbing. Quantified, the term "first class" may represent upwards of 10 but no more than 20 per cent of their number.'

No doubt the derisory practice of perpetuating traditional company hierarchies has contributed to a lowering of standards in chairmanship and a shortage of people developing skills suited to a specific career in that role. These shortcomings, plus a measure of chief executive power seeking, are mainly responsible for the continued attraction of the dual function.

The resulting downsides of duality are excessive power concentration with its baron-and-serf syndrome, a board weakened through imposed bias in agendas, discussion and decisions, lack of accountability in chief executive performance, attempts at fusion in one person of the incompatible or counterbalancing aspects of both roles, and the problem in firing the incumbent without an acrimonious struggle. In these circumstances a non-executive has difficulty in demonstrating independence either before being appointed or subsequently as part of his or her contribution. Nevertheless, non-executive directors often have a successful impact on their boards, bring about considerable change and prove to be of great value even against such odds.

Full-time chairman

In companies where duality is not followed, only a minority, about a third, of chairmen expect their duties to demand virtually the whole of their time. For the reasons we have seen, it is not difficult to imagine this being the case in a large, complex and widespread group or when a chairman is heavily committed to strategic, acquisitive or similar specific issues.

When deciding upon the contribution a chairman should make, it seems, a sensible arrangement to forgo rigid demarcation lines in favour of a dynamic-duo approach which divides the overall responsibilities in a way that fully uses the talents of both chief executive and chairman. Figure 5.1 is a demonstration assessment which shows how the two roles may be divided.

Unless sufficient tasks exist, as they might in a multinational for instance, it is difficult to imagine how a chairman could, let alone should, be fruitfully occupied full time when a chief executive is also in place. If a chairman has time to spare, or cares not to let go of the reins, he or she may negotiate an arrangement with the chief executive which allows considerable latitude in the running of the business. This is likely to be effective only if relationships are unusually strong, and success is almost always dependent upon acquiescence by the chief executive.

Comment

'If a chairman does not get out and about, involved elsewhere than in his own company,

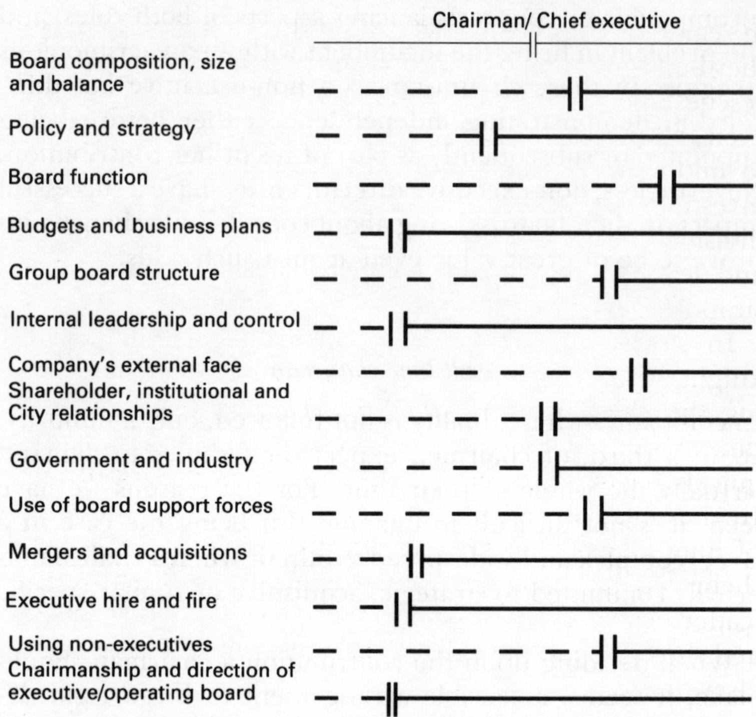

Figure 5.1 Division of responsibility between chairman and chief executive

> he quickly goes stale. His input becomes less effective, his learning curve flattened.'

Non-executives have a responsibility to encourage their chairman to be active and to have a portfolio of outside interests. These are essential to continued high performance, and such a dialogue is an important part of the relationship between chairman and non-executives.

Knight-errant chairman

This is a medieval title, close to present-day reality, for the many individuals who choose to wander the business fields in search of courageous deeds to do. Like Lewis Robertson, they build a reputation through a series of dramatic company rescues and command swift attention by their presence, or even the threat of it. Invariably called upon at five minutes to midnight by banks, a group of shareholders or major investing institutions, their brief is usually concise: avoid disaster, cut out disease, revive, restructure, regain impetus and leave in the capable hands of a chief executive and support team.

In a class apart from the normal troubleshooter, the knight-errant chairman takes total control, sometimes wearing the chief executive mantle, but only temporarily for time is short. Old-guard non-executives usually disappear quickly having accounted for their actions, or lack of them. In these liability prone days, even though attributing lack of due diligence is fraught with difficulty, life for some of them may never be quite the same again as other business leaders will assess their performance, even if only by hearsay and those judged to be inadequate are unlikely to be invited elsewhere.

As restructuring takes place, new non-executives are wheeled in to restore the company's credibility and help the body corporate to breathe again. Chances of total recovery now rest with the new chief executive and the part-time chairman successor to our knight-errant who, job done, moves on, with a purse which fully justifies the encounter.

Part-time chairman

In companies which separate the roles of chairman and chief executive, almost half ask their chairmen to act on a part-time basis. The proportion is slowly growing and is, as one might expect, significantly higher in large companies or those with an above average size of board.

As the title implies, each commitment is less than full time. Except for small businesses it generally involves between thirty and ninety days a year and is one of a range of interests. Appointees with a faculty for the role tend to centre their careers around the boardroom, have other non-executive or chairman appointments with unrelated companies and understand how to make good use of their non-executive directors.

However, the part-time role can also present a convenient step for those who are well advanced towards semi-retirement and its accompanying attitudes of mind. Taking the chair is sometimes seen as a right exclusive to former chief executives, or a prize given in recognition of a sizeable stakeholding or to a family successor, or worse still as another addition to the portfolio of a professional 'name'. Such interpretations of the role of part-time chairman are likely to have disastrous consequences.

When, on the other hand, chairmen are drawn from a range of people, perhaps in their late forties or fifties and clearly of pre-retirement age, they can frequently demonstrate skill and experience in the role:

- Having an unusually high degree of understanding of the range of duties and responsibilities of a chairman.
- Knowing why some chairmen are effective whereas others are undistinguished or lamentably fail to make any impact on board affairs.
- Having a blend of natural talent and developed ability in the role.
- Being prepared to put those talents to the test by making their commitment to the role of chairman an integral part of their continuing mainstream career.

The most significant rationale behind a chairman's multi-role career, however, is the better performance which results from the chairman's involvement in a number of separate activities outside the company. Wider perceptions and balanced attitudes offset the hazard of single company experience, which may otherwise make them blinkered in outlook.

Compare the chairmen, X and Y, of two medium-sized companies. X has a range of interests which include non-executive commitments with two unrelated companies, one being a group with European and US interests. She is also chairman of a smaller fast-moving enterprise and serves on two industry enterprise/training boards. Y confines his interests to related commercial matters, apart from which the company is his sole focus of attention. The difference in outlook and performance must be considerable, both in personal terms and in board performance.

The opportunity for the chairman to gain broad exposure is one of the crucial reasons for separating the roles of chairman and chief executive. With dual responsibility the experience of the office-holder is restricted. Although input from the non-executive directors should help open new horizons to the board, it is a chairman's receptive attitude which will influence how these possibilities are developed – ideally a board needs both.

The conclusions are clear. Look outside amongst busy people for the next part-time chairman. Because demand continues to outstrip supply and drawing up a specification is far from an exact science, it can be a convoluted and frustrating process. Non-executives are a useful source of advice both in taking an objective view of the search target and in assessing candidates. It is dangerous to leave selection solely in the hands of the chief executive.

Non-executive chairman

The term 'non-executive chairman' is gradually falling out of use as it becomes generally recognised that even the simplest version of a chairman's role has executive content. Meeting a company's legal obligations, presenting its external face, organising, staffing and running the board are just some of the basics – not to mention hiring or firing the chief executive. Suggestions that the role could be confined to scheduled meetings, AGMs, EGMs and 'Christmas hand shaking' either demonstrate complete naïvety or imply power domination from other quarters.

If the board wishes its chairman to be purely a 'name' or 'front person', then the title at least is appropriate, but non-executives who condone the practice rather than the misnomer really do have to question their continued existence, unless of course they also see their own function in similar terms. Many a chief executive and board of co-directors choose not to pursue the pretence and finally compromise with duality.

Without readily available guidance on the recruitment process this is hardly surprising. Nothing could be more off-putting than the miserable prospect of having a chairman whose function is simply to chair meetings, who remains aloof from any scene of creative activity and whose annual highlight is the AGM when, with a prepared script, the necessary formalities are conducted in a dignified monotone before a packed audience of less than a dozen. On such occasions it is amusing to note the supporting director chorus line, avidly following each word from copies of the written text, nodding, proposing and seconding on cue – even turning pages with such split-second timing that one cannot fail to be impressed by their unity of purpose.

> **Comment**
> A self-styled non-executive chairman, when asked what he did to motivate his non-executive directors, replied: 'Unlike executives who underperform, poor non-executives do little harm and they cost little, therefore one can afford to put up with them.'

There is not much that one can add to this pathetic statement, although the executives who had to suffer both 'seatwarmers' and chairman might have a word or two to offer on the subject!

THE CHAIRMAN AS AN AGENT OF CHANGE

Probably the best illustration of a new chairman's resolve is to be found in the changes in board size and composition or in group structure which follow within three to six months of appointment. In the case of the TSB, the thirty-strong main board was cut to half that number and over a hundred other board members were thought dispensable in a basic 'reawakening' programme initiated by the chairman, Sir Nicholas Goodison, within his first 'hundred days'.

The lasting imprint of change initiated by a chairman is evident. Roy Watts at Thames Water, the ebullient Sir John Harvey-Jones at ICI, Christopher Stewart-Smith at Conder, Sir Jeffrey Sterling at P&O and Professor Roland Smith almost everywhere are among scores of examples of a distinctively executive role being exercised with character, resolution and great skill. The catalytic, creative and forceful style of these chairmen may become contagious. A company does not have to be magnum size either to warrant such change or to appoint a chairman with the vision and ability to be as effective. Co-directors who persist in the belief that in the long term everything will be all right, even though the board presently shambles along and the chairman is really past his prime, will have an unpleasant surprise when a bid lands on the table.

And it is not just the boardroom shake-down that matters. The real benefits begin to flow when these changes in formation and attitudes at the top begin to work, as they must, through the lower echelons of the organisation.

OFFSETTING WEAKNESS IN THE CHAIRMAN

It would tie the chairman/non-executive relationship into a neat package if it were possible to plug the vulnerable gaps in a chairman's expertise with compensating values imported through the non-executives. It works rather well provided there are not too many gaps to plug and the chairman continues to run the board – it is all part of having a proper balance of skills and abilities around the board table. Unfortunately, if shortcomings are continually exposed, authority will be eroded and co-directors will look to the chief executive or one of the non-executives for board leadership. In such a situation opposing factions can easily develop and we often read press reports of the results. As a prescriptive approach to state-of-the-art boardroom practice it has these obvious flaws. Nevertheless, variations on this theme happen each day; astute chairmen are fully aware of their shortcomings and use their non-executives accordingly.

CHANGING THE CHAIRMAN

Comment
A quartet of comments worth remembering are:
'Powerful chairmen create weak boards.'
'Heavyweight chairmen – over the hill, go down fast.'
'Weak chairmen – a time-wasting liability.'
'Effective chairmen lift both board and company.'

Changing a chairman is a critical issue, far and away more important than changing any other director except a chief executive. When planned, agreed and publicised ahead of time, the success of transition rests on promoting incoming advantages while at least maintaining existing credibility and relationships.

Effecting a reluctant departure is another matter, especially when it follows internal friction if not downright combat. When a chairman, for whatever reason, needs to be replaced yet is reluctant even to contemplate going, the task of arranging his or her removal often falls to the non-executives. Generally they act as a body, although one of them may take the lead.

Individual hint-dropping sorties seldom lead to anything, and subterfuge fares little better. Chairmen may in time lose most of their faculties but guile is often the last to go.

Comment
'We decided the best means of getting rid of our cantankerous old chairman was to reduce the retirement age of directors from

> seventy to sixty-two. It was duly proposed and he agreed. We were delighted even though some of our own expectations were shortened. Then, with an ill-concealed twinkle he turned to the Secretary and said, "First-class idea, record a unaminous decision, but remember to note that this does not, of course, apply to chairmen.'"

Non-executives need to be sure that their proposals are valid and that the subsequent implications are fully understood. Each non-executive should be:

- Resolved about the need for change and the benefits to board and company which will result.
- Clear about who will be the successor, when and why, or alternatively how a successor can be found.
- Mindful of the degree of thought, care and time involved.
- Agreed that the financial package for both incoming and outgoing chairman is fair and its terms soundly based.
- Confident that his or her own unbiased opinions will stand the test of critical or coercive attack by either the chairman or any co-director.
- Prepared to act in concert with other non-executives should the need arise and to defend their actions in the light of external publicity.

Change, some call it evolution, is swiftly brought about when all six criteria are met, but in practice it seldom happens that way. Most of the issues become clouded by genuine differences of opinion, personal allegiance, comfort with current results or reluctance to rock the boat.

If the non-executive is solo, from the outset the chances of effecting change are slim. The prospect of mounting a one-person crusade in the face of considerable resistance may prove too strong a deterrent. Wise heads on experienced shoulders might advise that working to strengthen the non-executive presence is a better initial objective. Whichever is chosen, to act and fail will invite retribution or disaster, or both. Failure to act at all raises the question as to whether the continued existence of the non-executive director is justified. If loyalty and support for the chairman cannot be combined with an acknowledged right to assert independence should the need arise, a non-executive quickly becomes a mere pawn in the game.

> **Comment**
> 'The lesson I draw from the twenty-odd years that I was an "outside director" is that the position of a non-executive director, and to a degree that of the chairman, is untenable unless he, or she, is supported by a core of independently minded non-executive colleagues who can stand aloof from the play for personal power which takes place round all board tables. Needless to say, the building of such a core is an extremely difficult task.'

WHO REGULATES THE BOARD?

During the past fifty years the pendulum of ownership has swung dramatically from a majority holding by private investors to dominance by institutional shareholders, in particular the life insurance companies and pension funds. In neither instance is the owner generally seen as able to exert meaningful pressure on the boards of companies in which it invests, preferring discreet back-stage discussions to lively interrogation at the allotted AGM platforms. The latter, as a result, remain dull events, thinly populated with greying heads who listen to a ritual of irrelevant platitudes or nervous questioning.

Two evergreen statements are almost guaranteed not to arouse curiosity as to the speaker's motives, yet they echo daily in a hundred or more boardrooms and at nearly as many annual general meetings: 'British companies need less, not more regulating'; 'Your board is acting with experience and sound judgement in the best interests of you, the shareholders, who together own this great company'. The chairman usually takes the honour for such quotations and often both may be said on the same occasion, perhaps achieving the ultimate in mythological bromides. By a strange coincidence, however, when combined they pinpoint a key aspect of each non-executive's responsibility, namely: to ensure that the necessary degree of collective self-regulation exists within the board so that it acts in good faith, with loyalty, care and skill towards and in the interests of the company – and all that implies.

David Walker's reported comment that 'British executive management is less accountable than any other in the leading Western industrial countries' is absolutely right. External pressures applied by the Bank of England and other institutions may in time change the climate of opinion, and recent Company's Acts stiffen the penalties for misdemeanour. Nevertheless, it remains the case that a board where ineffectiveness, overmanning and restrictive practices abound and whose members are absorbed with self-interest is unlikely to improve unless change is brought about from within.

Applying self-regulation demands all a chairman's skill and personal standing. The chairman runs the board and therefore its actions clearly come within the chairman's jurisdiction, regardless of whether or not the role is combined with that of chief executive. If a chairman does not know what the board is doing, or does not care to know, or shies away from putting his or her authority to the test – and is either content or allowed to continue in office – then all the regulation in the world will be of little avail. That is probably why the job is so difficult to do, and why so few people perform it well.

Comment
The words of Eldridge Cleaver, without having chairmen specifically in mind, are perhaps of singular relevance to them: 'You're either part of the problem, or part of the solution.'

Initiators of the solution chairmen frequently are. I have worked on boardroom matters with over two hundred chairmen, and the majority clearly took a positive and responsible attitude to their duties. Perhaps because they were already taking steps to develop their boards, however, this sample was not representative. Without their progressive attitude it would have been pointless to embark upon the time-consuming processes of reviewing board make-up, balance and function, let alone examine benefits from introducing independent non-executives who could add weight to the concept of self-regulation.

Chairmen who are openly prepared to review their board, and in so doing themselves, either fully appreciate their role or intend to sharpen their mastery of it. The remainder, for whatever reason, may not be so enthusiastic about exposing their provinces to an outsider unless forcefully nudged by imminent stock market requirements, a powerful individual or worried institutional shareholders.

To strike a judicious balance between numbers of chairmen who fall into the 'problem' and 'solution' categories is far from easy; certainly 'problems' carry the day, perhaps by as many as two to one.

> **Comment**
> 'Then the — Company; here we had the worst of all arrangements in that the non-executives were mostly self-important has-beens with the inevitable knighthood or peerage. They were condescending in their attitude to the executives, giving no effective contribution to the company, and very largely traded on the company to support their reputations. The principal reason for their appointment was "I'll scratch your back if you'll scratch mine", and a reasonably incompetent chairman was immune from criticism by appointing the directors to, in turn, support him in the most absurd business situations.'

If the chairman in the above case had not been incompetent, it is unlikely that such a comment would have been made. Consider the ways in which, from your own experience, chairman appointments have come about, and reflect upon the results which followed.

CONCLUSION

Drawing together the nature of the job and the way it is normally carried out, it is difficult to avoid the conclusion that chairmen present the weakest link in the chain which should bind all directors in common purpose around the boardroom table. But why should such a statement be made in a book about non-executive directors? Simply because:

- It is not good enough to focus on deficiencies or attributes or the potential value of non-executives without a similar examination of their chairmen.
- Chairmanship is the one function which, more than any other, determines the quality of the non-executive element in a board and the relationships of non-executives with co-directors and senior management.
- A chairman controls non-executive and board performance.

When one stops to consider the customary ways in which chairmen are appointed, it is arguable that no other freely made business decisions are based on such a diversity of reasons which are irrelevant or defy sound commercial logic. Part-time outsider chairmen are scarce birds, or so it seems, for companies of all sizes find difficulty in attracting someone who is at all competent in that role. However, those who succeed are encouraged by results and the word is spreading.

Recently, the much-vaunted notion of reskilling has been applied to a variety of people with limited or outmoded skills, so why not have a reskilling programme for chairmen? This proposal will, I hope, find support in Sir Adrian Cadbury's forthcoming book *The Company Chairman* (Director Books, 1990).

One project which may work is being initiated by the Institute of Directors. They have accepted the challenge of the chairman problem as part of their current surge to improve professional standards and the competence of directors. New workshops, in-depth courses and a recommended code of practice are all in the pipeline. The Institute of Directors also plans to introduce a specific chairman appointments service during 1990.

It is a beginning, but the position is unlikely to change radically until the Bank of England, the CBI, PRO NED, their governing bodies, sponsors and supporters take off their blinkers and, together with the Institute of Directors, publicise a new perception of the chairman's role and begin to place greater emphasis on putting the chairman's house in order, instead of concentrating on the numbers of non-executive lodgers they can persuade the chairman to allow into the boardroom.

6

Relating to the Chief Executive

Having a good memory is one of the more useful non-executive director qualities. It is not the power to recall minutiae which is important, but rather an aspect of memory which in some non-executives is subject to lapses of convenience. As they busily stoke rather than quell the fires that flicker beneath a chief executive's seat, they too easily forget what it was like to be in the hot seat themselves.

It is surprising how quickly attitudes harden and the term 'close monitoring of management performance' becomes a suitable opportunity to second-guess or criticise the chief executive. Non-executive directors who are themselves running an unrelated company do not suffer from this flaw, which is perhaps a strong reason for their popularity. This in no way suggests that a non-executive director must have chief executive experience to qualify for the role, but in one context or another each non-executive should be an achiever in his or her own right, should know what the hot seat feels like – and remember.

UNDERSTANDING

A chief executive's job tops the management pyramid. It is unquestionably the greatest individual business opportunity, and its demands on the time, personal qualities and stamina of the holder are quite unlike those of any other role. There is need for a special degree of understanding by co-directors not only in relating to an operational chief executive, but also in choosing the right person for the job. Non-executive directors, who may be closely involved in selection, should recognise the motivations, personality and operating techniques which are characteristic of the role.

Excellence is usually self-evident. It is not difficult to welcome aboard a charismatic, entrepreneurial visionary who is determined to achieve success and who knows how to lead the team and the business through change, innovation and growth with professional panache. The problem is that such people are thin on the ground and that nearly all chief executive seats are occupied by mere mortals. So a non-executive has first to see how the company's perceived need is matched by the chief executive's particular mix of strengths and weaknesses, then decide what can be done to help fill the gaps.

Leaving aside the paragons, the following broad-brush illustrations show some of the variations in style and approach one might expect to find in a chief executive:

- The 'Taipan' or dynastic ruler whose progress towards the seat of power was irrevocably predestined in the minds of all, not least the chief executive's own share-controlling family.
- The long-term company executive of progressive, solid ability who knows the business backwards, is appointed on seniority and whose natural instinct is to plan an era of consolidated growth.
- The 'maverick' who, leapfrogging over the heads of others, has established a reputation based on quite radical and innovative propositions.
- The creative trading wizard who magically conceives new rules for the commercial game and exploits 'windows of opportunity' which others fail to see, but thereafter cannot manage projects in a way which transfers potential benefits to bottom-line profit.
- The smooth-talking, smart financier who achieved control through bringing a backed minority shareholding

through the side door, is busy overworking asset credibility to boost share price in the short term, and will soon be casting around for a suitable exit.

- The bullish appointee from outside who has climbed up the executive ladder through a series of larger companies and for the first time is taking the pivot position.
- The single-minded careerist to whom everything and everybody serves as a means to an end and who rides this corporate vehicle because success will further enhance a growing reputation.
- The seasoned professional who has experienced both success and failure in the role. A journeyman chief executive with faith in organisation and the use of conventional management skills.
- The rising and favoured company star whose combative style inhibits dissent or even rational discussion on almost any issue.
- The established VIP whose engagement deal is conditional upon securing a hefty chunk of the equity. A chief executive whose City *savoir-faire* attracts block shareholders, investing institutions, bankers and stockbrokers whose views seem to be given precedence over those of co-directors. With almost hypnotic ease the board is propelled through a zero-option programme of disposals and acquisitions.

All of these types could in their own fashion be good news for a company, but only one is likely to match its immediate needs. In assessing the suitability of either the present incumbent or the proposed successor, a non-executive cannot sit on the fence and reserve judgement while the company chairman and co-directors make the running.

Given reasonable freedom, it is arguable that a chief executive's influence on events within a company is as great as the combined input of the chairman and all the co-directors. Without fully understanding the person and role of the chief executive, a non-executive's impact on board and company is inevitably lightweight.

Protection

It may seem odd, and in a sense perhaps it is, to cast the non-executive as the protector of the chief executive, especially as this function involves protecting a chief executive as much from himself or herself as from others. However, although few dispute the importance attached to a chief executive position regardless of the size or status of company, surprisingly enough in many instances the opportunity for the chief executive to succeed is either lost or prejudiced within the first hundred days in office.

To be effective an able chief executive needs an equally effective board. Too often the chief executive is carried away by the sheer exhilaration of the moment, compromising the future by accepting a misalliance among board colleagues or agreeing to unnecessary constraints on freedom to operate. For example, how many chief executives:

- Put up with a chairman who still wants to run things, is in office through expedience and not merit, or is gently submerging into retirement?
- Are prepared to work with a board composition which is so cluttered with biased non-executive directors and leftovers from yesterday as to be virtually unworkable, or, worse still, try to counter such a parasitical arrangement by creating a cadre of executives who make all the decisions, leaving the formal board meeting as a rubber-stamping charade?
- Find the invitation to carry out a dual role so flattering or the temptation of power so great, that caution is thrown aside as they assume themselves suddenly to possess qualities which embrace the quite distinct chairman and chief executive functions?
- Are concerned less with a handsome pay-off for achieving specific goals than with a contract which provides vast sums in compensation if they fail and get fired?

On the other hand, how many chief executives:

- Ask for, and receive, lines of authority and responsibility clearly defined as between themselves and the board?
- Openly discuss their particular management style with all co-directors, and receive equally open support?

So, in almost no time at all, a chief executive can become locked in to a path which has to cross a minefield. From experience, non-executives should know of the dangers, and in fairness they should have helped clear a route for the newcomer whom they have a duty to protect.

> **Comment**
> A chairman said the following about his new 'cellular-linked' chief executive: 'It was at this point our contact and communications reached their best and highest level. Was it to impress me that he was on his way to the office, even as I drank my early morning cup of tea? It confirmed what I already suspected – our new MD was that fashionable thing, a workaholic!'

Chief executive, managing director or general manager?

Misunderstanding between titles is now minimal, although some companies still follow a policy which precludes anyone involved in management of the business from being a director, the most senior operating title being general manager. While this simplifies the separation of management from direction, which was its original purpose, it is not normal UK company practice.

In European two-tier structures the distinction is made by having two boards, the chief executive or general manager not being a member of the supervisory tier although available to attend its meetings if required. In Norway, for example, a company is run by a general manager who is not a director but who attends meetings of a totally non-executive board. This board averages six members and, in Scandinavian fashion, will include two employee representatives even when the company is quite small and total staff may not exceed thirty or forty.

In practice, titles make little difference to operational responsibilities. When disaster strikes it is invariably the general manager who either wins support for remedial action or is dismissed; it is rare for the supervisory board to go. An exception was the Statoil débâcle, an event which attracted the following press note, surely one of the year's least urbane comments: 'Management makes a critical difference in the ability of a company to function effectively in radically changing economic environments.'

THE FUNDAMENTAL CATALYST

A chief executive has an immense influence over the introduction and execution of change. A notable example is Tube Investments, a long-troubled group which housed a multiplicity of accumulated constraints. Now called TI, with Christopher Lewington at the helm, it has been transformed into a lean, vigorous and profitable company concentrating on becoming world leader in a few specialised engineering sectors. This quite remarkable change was highlighted by Harvard Business School, which chose to use it in its corporate renewal programme. It will be interesting to track TI's progress following Lewington's move from chief executive to chairman.

To bring about rapid change, an incoming chief executive can stimulate the attention of senior management and hasten their responses by the use of 'destabilising techniques'. Designed to create uncertainty, they involve what may at the time appear to be the indiscriminate disjointing of established management patterns coupled with the selective dismissal of one or more executives. In fact these are carefully planned steps in the process of introducing a new focal point for objectives and disciplines. This shock-treatment approach, with its attendant casualties, may be less than ideal, and non-executives applauding the resulting speed of change should be aware of both means and justification.

An alternative pressure-building technique is sometimes referred to as 'management by applied tension'. It again hinges on creating a degree of personal uncertainty far beyond anything normally exerted even in rigorous management. The ploy demands a chief executive of somewhat quirky mentality who can continually produce an icy gaze, or can deliver a threat at the end of almost every directive. Most often used by workaholics who lack the ability and humanity to lead from the front, sadly it often indicates an oddity in behaviour which could manifest itself in other directions.

Determined chief executives are not always totally rational beings. In full flight and with tail up, they are near invincible, but with confidence wavering, and short of the support and understanding of their colleagues, they are highly vulnerable and reactive to those within their closer circles. Each non-executive director will at times share some of the chief executive's frustrations or join in speculative think-tank or confidential sounding-board sessions. Though infrequent, these require all a non-executive's experience and judgement, and it is unforgivable not to sense the occasion and respond.

The shape of support

One principle is paramount: a chief executive needs a strong board, one which gives rather than receives direction and is demanding and supportive in full and equal measure. That message carries an unequivocal challenge for the non-executive director, who only exists by virtue of the contribution he or she makes to the board. When contemplating ways in which the chief executive, and therefore the company, can be supported, a non-executive should:

- Want the chief executive to be successful in job performance.
- Build a regular dialogue about the business and its progress.

- Be an occasional and useful sounding board, responding with both improvised and considered reactions.
- Take on special tasks which fit with personal know-how.
- Avoid putting the chief executive into battle without first having worked through and agreed the plan.
- Comment directly and frankly on achievements and failures.
- Listen but avoid being the centre of gossip.
- Promote attitudes of loyalty among co-directors, and question niggling dissenters, fence-sitters and snipers.
- At meetings be positive and say what is intended with due force, never allowing silence to be mistaken for acquiescence.
- When performance appears to be faltering, talk with the chairman, even if the chief executive is also the chairman.
- If change seems inevitable, take soundings from both chairman and other non-executive directors, and with consensus encourage action without delay.
- Help to ensure that the board appoints a new chief executive who is suited to the company's future needs, then show a commitment to make that incumbent successful.

These are only some of the opportunities, for so much depends on the type and size of company and, of course, on the people involved. But if the non-executive director feels uncomfortable with the whole idea of playing a supportive role, then in fairness to everyone it is better to ask the chairman to review the non-executive's contribution. Finding a replacement non-executive could be the solution.

The other side of the coin

Should non-executive directors ever entertain the idea that their chief executive will be eternally grateful for support, the delusion should be swiftly put aside. By their very nature chief executives are highly motivated and personally committed to drive a company forward with whatever degree of rigour the situation demands. This is not conducive to spontaneous bursts of gratitude or the development of highly compatible boardroom companions.

> **Comment**
> 'The boss, whoever that may be, is the one who will make or break the non-executives.'

The use of the term 'boss' is illuminating, since it usually indicates the seat of ultimate power regardless of title. It may describe the chairman or chief executive or someone who combines the roles, or could refer to a hand which pulls the levers under the guise of president or a family shareholding non-executive director.

> **Comment**
> 'A change at the top makes little difference; whoever runs the company will need the approval of the . . . family on major issues.'

Admittedly, situations such as that described are more likely to happen in a company which is private, but who cannot think of a public limited company where similar influences exist?

Direct confrontation between a chief executive and a non-executive director will invariably arise at some time or other during their relationship because each must constantly test the directional focus of the company and challenge existing concepts. It may happen in private discussion or across the board table, and may concern a point of policy, an imperious act, the explosion of pent-up feelings on petty issues, a suspected covert operation or seemingly unwarranted criticism. Either party can be the initiator and each occasion will rigorously test a non-executive's mettle. The board would be the poorer if these contentious issues failed to surface.

Leaving combative stances and power play aside, a chief executive's assessment of a non-executive director is not only crucial to their relationship but will also govern the degree of effective dialogue and support which they exchange.

Normally, opinions centre around personal respect and chemistry, the value of experience, contacts and commercial opinions, and usefulness in board or private discussion. If the conclusion is a negative judgement, the chief executive will probably concentrate on the following factors.

- Unrewarding use of executive time and effort to keep the non-executive informed.
- The level of the non-executive's independence or allegiance, and if the latter predominates, then to whom and why.
- The non-executive's policy bias, whether towards status quo or change and innovation.
- The non-executive's individual board standing and ability to persuade others.
- The willingness of the non-executive to act in concert with other non-executives: their potential collective power.
- The obstacles in the path of the non-executive's early removal.

A chief executive's interest in a non-executive director's motivations primarily derives not from kindly concern but rather from trying to deduce whether at board level the non-executive is likely to back executive programmes or to scatter unnecessary obstacles in their path. One major advantage a unitary board has over its current two-tier alternative is the regular opportunity its meetings provide for non-executives to work face to face and establish a dialogue with the chief executive – and in the process to agree parameters for boardroom harmony and the avoidance of debilitating friction.

The boardroom may begin to sound like a battlefield; in practice, however, relationships usually work out rather well, especially once a semblance of pecking order is established. If a company is to be led by professional and competent executives who are committed to success, then blunt dialogue will predominate over fanciful innuendoes, and a passive state of boardroom peace and tranquillity will not break out too often – or for too long. Non-executives would be naïve to think otherwise, or doomed if unable to stand their ground and match skills during the cut and thrust of debate.

> **Comment**
> A chief executive said the following after an exploratory meeting with a prospective non-executive: 'Quite splendid, a delightful and most experienced chap who would be a real asset to our board, except we could never live with his confounded impeccability, and he would be left speechless by the manner of our behaviour, one to another, let alone the language we use.'

Good times are not isolated occasions and they come in abundance when the whole board generates a clear, creative and effective impetus. For the non-executive director this objective form of experience in corporate governance is a unique chance to gain a broader perspective on ways to tackle the perpetual challenge of success in business life.

RELATING PAYMENT TO PERFORMANCE

'Achievement justifies reward' is the theme of today's enterprise culture. If we are to continue to breed successive generations of dynamic executives, their motivations will need to be honed with tools more apt than a stick and carrot.

Relatively few companies fail to provide a fringe-benefit package to their chief executive and functional heads, but on average these are worth no more than twenty-five per cent of basic, plus an incentive element of about half that sum. Compared to the influence these executives have on results, the amounts received pay little more than lip service to the notion of incentives and are so paltry that it is arguable a greater incentive lies in failure. 'Get more if I'm kicked out' was a somewhat cynical but apt comment. Almost every day we read of astounding sums being paid as gratuities on leaving, firing pay-offs, exit sweeteners or silence conditioners.

Timid performance payment schemes repeatedly dissuade chief executives from pursuing longer-term careers as top-flight company leaders. In the hope of making a fortune in double-quick time, many move on to a wheeler-dealer track used by high-wire financial acrobats.

To be fully effective, rewards must reach far beyond a stereotype or notional annual bonus. It is becoming accepted that a caucus of independent non-executive directors, looking at performance-related payments with commercial objectivity, are ideally suited to offer adventurous, some may even suggest audacious, proposals to the executive. Working in this way, it is possible to foster enterprise-related attitudes throughout an organisation.

It is a vital part of the role of non-executive directors to breathe new life into countless mundane remuneration committees and, in so doing, to create a 'state of the art' in the design of a corporate culture which links people to acceptance of risks, pride of performance, readily perceived status, financial payment and an enhanced quality of life.

Industrial and commercial leaders are responsible for the wealth, employment and security of substantial sectors of the community. Without promoting personal greed or the culture of modern Pharisees, both targets and rewards need to be high. Over a dozen executives now achieve total packages valued in excess of £1 million, another thirty over £500,000 and many hundreds more in excess of £100,000. Coupled with improved public relations, plus a dash of personality cultism, top jobs in commerce and industry are now able to compete with both the City and the professions. In the process they have also begun to put the Atlantic brain drain into reverse.

CONCLUSION

The relationship between non-executive and chief executive should be one of the most enjoyable and fruitful in the boardroom and it very often is. At times each has to bend a little – of the two, the non-executive should have greater natural aptitude and skill to encourage and guide the process.

> **Comment**
> A chairman said the following of his chief executive: 'His answers did not reveal a breadth of knowledge nor particular intellectual capacity, rather the quality of a man who knew where he wanted to go, and if he couldn't find the key to a given door would get in through the window.'

When skilful, and with efforts well spent, non-executives hold and can turn the key to this door.

7

Non-Executives and the Board

A company is an intangible legal entity, a business enterprise in which shareholders invest money – short or long term – to make money. As owners, they offset some practical limitations on their authority to control against the benefits of having a limit to their financial and legal liability. The guardians of the owners' interests are an assembly of people who are the company's governors, or its board, and who direct its affairs. As directors, there is no limit to their individual or collective liability and there is seldom a limit to their ambitions for power, fortune and survival.

The boardroom is usually where directors meet to consider, decide and direct how management should deal with the company's present and future business. But a boardroom is essentially mobile, for directors do meet in a variety of locations – and for a variety of purposes. At times their quite ruthless struggle for power means that discussions in such meeting places often include the well-being, or otherwise, of colleagues.

Shareholders have the power to appoint or dismiss a director although it is seldom exercised in quoted plcs. Normally a director is appointed by the board, and shareholders formally approve by electing the appointee through a resolution at the next AGM – and re-elect each subsequent third year if the incumbent and co-directors wish that office to continue. Board action to dismiss a director usually emerges in the civilised guise of resignation accompanied, where a chairman or executive director is concerned, by a negotiated settlement. Unless specified in the company's

Articles, or otherwise agreed – as might be the case in a subsidiary company, for example – a non-executive cannot be forced to resign, or be dismissed, except by a meeting of shareholders. Without the goodwill of others around the boardroom table it is an arduous experience for a non-executive to remain a director as either a considered duty or on technical grounds, yet surprisingly it happens frequently.

This chapter intends to provide an uncustomary view of the board function, to highlight where the action now happens and to identify changes in board concepts which non-executive directors will face within the next five years.

Accepted definitions can sometimes be misleading. In a recent questionnaire, the prescribed answer to 'What is a director?' was 'One amongst equals in the boardroom.' On the face of it there can be little argument with that, except in the way one interprets the word 'equal'. It clearly refers to the shared or collective responsibility of all directors, but some play a special role. Equality could never apply to the degree of influence exercised by one or two members of the board in either the build-up to decision making, or the rapid dispatch of a less favoured alternative.

> **Comment**
> 'Autonomy is what you take, not what you are given.'

THE BOARD'S ROLE

It is worth looking briefly at the unitary board's primary functions, for which all members carry a responsibility. These are to:

- Nominate directors, elect a chairman and appoint the chief executive.
- Set objectives, define policy and develop strategy.
- Interpret corporate culture, ethical standards and people rationale into everyday acts.

- Specify authorities of chairman, chief executive and board.
- Make certain the chief executive provides satisfactory leadership, planning, organisation, control and succession.
- Approve short- and medium-term plans: tactical, technical, operational and financial.
- Monitor performance against agreed goals.
- Check that employees, customers, suppliers and society get a fair deal from the company and that a proper balance exists between their interests and those of shareholders.
- Account to shareholders for the results.
- Recommend distribution of profits.
- Ensure present plans and actions provide for the company's continuity.
- When necessary, remove the chairman or, through the chairman, the chief executive or executive directors.

Each of these functions is an integral part of the total decision-making process. If the directors fail to perform in even one area, the subsequent operational task of management cannot be fully effective.

The list shows the span of board inputs expected of non-executive directors as key contributors. To expect any individual to play a prominent part in them all is clearly a tall order, but when shared between the complementary strengths of two or three non-executives, their fulfilment is a practical possibility.

Perhaps two aspects deserve particular emphasis in relation to directors' shared responsibility and the non-executives' overall monitoring function: ethics and decision making.

Ethical Standards

Superimposed upon all the collective skills and abilities of a board is its acknowledgement of a fundamental moral philosophy. Standards in a company are first set and practised by its directors. A unified approach is necessary if an inherent code of corporate ethics is to run through an organisation from its chairman to its most recent recruit. Issuing memos which pay lip service to the notion or setting new rules for the buying office are only gestures.

Each non-executive needs not only to have a clear picture of the moral values in question but also to be known, and seen, to apply them personally as a way of promoting their acceptance by co-directors. While exemplary ethics in no way guarantee right decision making, a board so unified appears to operate faster and with less friction between the component parts. When mistrust, backbiting and covert discussions make up an unwritten shadow agenda, frustration and disappointing results are likely to follow.

Decision making

Board decisions which have a dramatic and lasting impact upon a company's future happen on only two or three occasions in each decade. Changes in destiny therefore usually arise from:

- An accumulation of relatively small, unrelated and ill-considered judgements.
- The 'knock-on' multiplicative effect of pursuing a line of action based upon a fundamental misconception which is never subsequently challenged.
- Allowing the stream of information about competitors to run dry.
- Working in blinkers towards an objective which is outdated by social, political or market trends.
- Unquestioning allegiance to directives from a single source.
- Being unaware of the need for constant innovative change.
- In plcs, remaining inactive while the 'value gap' (the difference between market capitalisation and asset value)

widens, exposing an irresistable underbelly to one of the roaming predators.

In the current era, when financial speculators dominate the equity market, all quoted companies need to know the possible sources from which the next bid, merger, buy-out or buy-in may be launched, either in their direction or at another in their commercial sector. These used not to be regular items on the agenda, but few plc boards now meet without these activities being featured. Unquoted companies enjoy comparative security but are not immune to the temptation to succumb to or even flirt outrageously with suitor and saviour alike.

In the build-up to decision time and at the crucial event, non-executives with broad experience in corporate policy making play an invaluable part in a board's deliberations, which often run over a period of weeks rather than days. Seasoned directors know that most policy decisions are resolved in any one of half a dozen locations outside the designated boardroom, even though that is where the final act may take place.

ASSESSING DIFFERENT BOARD CONCEPTS

Comment
'A board has to continually evolve in line with the changing needs and circumstances of the company. An executive's life span may be seven years and a non-executive's even less. Regular changes in both are necessary to sustain a climate of vigour and innovation.'

Before responding to even preliminary overtures about joining a board, prospective non-executives should have a clear mind as to the board concept which they feel is most naturally akin to their own contributory style. When an approach materialises, prospective non-executives are well advised to research the characteristics of the board they are being asked to join. The following variations may help to establish suitable benchmarks.

The small company unitary board

Unsurprisingly perhaps, over ninety-seven per cent of all companies are small and, particularly in early life, have an all-executive board which does not meet in the formal sense of creating policy and giving direction. If it does, the directors will usually focus upon the immediate problems facing the business. In what is sure to be a strongly management-oriented dialogue, it is arguable that these are the key issues anyway and that, at that stage of development, taking time for other relatively sophisticated matters would be an ill-afforded luxury.

This short-term operational focus often delays the use of even one non-executive and therefore the formation of a true board. Likened to a stranger in their midst, a non-executive director may be seen as too great a psychological hurdle for a close-knit, buoyant executive team. Many long-serving directors consider that any proposal to bring in an outsider directly at board level almost defies natural justice and circumvents years of hard graft up the management pyramid, its pinnacle still thought to be embodied in a seat on the board.

Perhaps the difficulty of making such a fundamental change to established practice is one reason why many proprietorial company owners choose to invite an ex-professional adviser, or a business or personal friend to be their first non-executive. They are people with whom the senior management has become well acquainted over the years, their contribution will be respected, they pose no threat to existing lines of authority – and from the owners' viewpoint they are unlikely to rock the boat. Frequently the expected contribution is not sustained and the non-executive turns native, finding it easier or more stimulating to join the mêlée dealing with almost routine problems of management.

Introducing the first independent non-executive director into a comparatively immature board requires full use of a chairman's skills and the co-operation of owners and all directors. The cautious early months often bring evident benefits in the style and conduct of meetings which reflect the concentration of minds on issues of direction.

The non-executive at this stage takes on an almost dual role, giving of his or her best without either becoming an arbitrator between factions or unsurping the chairman's co-ordinating function. At the same time the non-executive should coach and encouraging colleagues to join in thinking the unthinkable, responding to or even leap-frogging beyond the catalytic views of others while at the same time applying the questioning mental disciplines and new horizons required of a director. Being independent and an outsider may make the process easier, but success will require the full employment of the non-executive's boardroom experience.

Comment
'Unless heading for "market", the full-time directors of companies with a turnover of less than £6–8 million have difficulty in coming to terms with the independent director's role. Even though not involved in day-to-day executive decisions, it helps resolve these doubts if non-executive directors bring some specific skill to the party, skills that could help improve performance, perhaps in the area of corporate planning, finance or broad marketing strategy.'

The unitary boards of medium and larger companies

Years ago, Professor Joad might have said, 'It depends what you mean by unitary.' Now, one could equally say, 'It depends how you see the board.' To limit one's view to an omniscient group which meets periodically to determine the fortunes of a company, its owners and its staff is in itself ill-judged. The boardroom should be the culmination of perceived company knowledge, like the control capsule in a space rocket.

Established boards in the United Kingdom are typically unitary in style and have between five and twelve directors, of whom a quarter to a third carry a non-executive label. In its democratic form, the prescription which appears to bring best results is a combination of:

- Chairman's guidance and co-ordination.
- Chief executive's leadership and single-minded drive.
- Independent non-executive's experience, complementary skills and judgement.
- Executive's technical know-how and close understanding of practical implications.
- Support groups drawn from:
  divisions or subsidiary company boards;
  professional advisers from the legal, accountancy, banking, public relations and City institutional sectors;
  specialist consultants;
  line management and employee task forces.

The aim is to produce a totally integrated view and culture in order to:

- Shape the company's destiny.
- Achieve profit.
- Improve the quality of life for everyone directly or indirectly associated with the company.

Boards are found not to function so well when their operating formula allows impediments such as:

- Overmanning and restrictive practices amongst directors in the boardroom.
- A chairman who is retired in mind and only marking time for a pension.
- Dependence on a single person for policy, drive and decision making.

- Friction and sniping between an old-guard and a new-style management.
- Employees deprived of leadership, vision, challenge and a sense of purpose.
- Long-tenancy non-executive seat-warmers who occasionally rumble like expiring volcanoes.
- Support groups frustrated by indecision and lack of positive action.

An independent non-executive is invited, not coerced, to join a board. In that respect the non-executive is a free agent and thus able to exercise a particular influence in a unitary board. To savour the experience of contributing within a democratic board, without impediments, is exhilarating not just for the non-executive but for everyone; it is also rare and may only happen for two or three short periods during a business life.

Under other regimes within the unitary concept the immediate prospects facing an incoming non-executive may be somewhat daunting; their challenge is a test not so much of confidence but of a non-executive's self-analysis in recognising responsive personal characteristics.

The feudal board

The United Kingdom represents a strange paradox: internationally recognised as a people prepared actively to uphold democratic rights no matter what the cost, yet nationally almost passive in accepting that those who rule the majority of UK companies still cling to a near-medieval feudal culture. The 'baron', whether owner, chairman or chief executive claims the right not only to dominate the present but also to predestine the line of succession. It is an attitude where leadership towards future objectives is considered secondary to an impregnable power base.

In keeping with true Anglo-Saxon landowning traditions, there are few equals to the power attached to the ownership of 'property', albeit in its broadest sense. The roles of baron and serf are re-enacted in countless boardrooms and businesses each day, a high proportion of which, through their participation in the market-place, are in essence no longer part of a personal or family domain.

In this environment it is perhaps surprising to find that non-executive directors who are prepared to express forthright independent views often enjoy a princely status and make a contribution to match. Others carry the unseen shackles of too many years spent in full-time executive or professional servitude.

The board coterie

Few executives, or non-executives come to that, fail to be impressed by their own sense of importance when invited to enter the inner sanctum of power sharing. To be a member of the gang which manipulates the strings may impose a rigorous responsibility, but the warmth of being an 'insider' promotes an assured attitude which makes light of such tasks. One's conscience may suggest that all directors should be offered the chance to share that warmth – then all would respond accordingly. But that virtuous assumption requires not only an exceptional degree of equality but also a balance in personal chemistry which is rarely found in either small partnerships or a conclave of cardinals, let alone amongst co-directors.

This 'board within a board' concept often works in spite of its apparent injustice. Perhaps it is the lesser of two evils, since boards can all too easily become bogged down by executives and non-executives who are there for reasons other than merit of contribution. Such appointees predictably show a marked degree of willingness, if not eagerness, to abdicate their responsibilities as directors, to stand back from the cut and thrust of debate and so avoid being measured too closely.

Sometimes the vacuum so created is never filled and the board flounders on regardless, but frustration usually brings forward a standard-bearer for change, even if it manifests itself in covert plotting for power. Alternatively, a non-executive may try to counter the inertia by stimulating non-executive colleagues to form a 'critical mass' of objective independent opinion to initiate action through the existing chairman – although finding a successor might be more fruitful. In all these gyrations the non-executives must, of course, avoid the trap of forming yet another coterie.

> **Comment**
> 'The most critical issue in the boardrooms of most companies is the relationship between chairman, managing director and finance director.'

The executive board

Although a board consisting only of executives may also be subject to feudal influences, or nurture its own coterie, there is patently less pretence surrounding the process. Executives live each day within a power structure and learning the pecking order is an early discipline not easily forgotten.

Understandably most prefer an all-executive board where the status quo is retained. Once outsiders are introduced in the form of non-executives, meetings become less comfortable, equality around the table an esoteric concept and often, under a chief executive's dominant presence, free expression inhibited.

> **Comment**
> A laconic Texan said the following: 'When I get a new "chief" who is a bow-legged swine, there is no point in getting uptight about the situation. I absorb the bastard and bide my time – it seldom comes, but I'm alive today to tell the tale.'

Executive boards, when they have accomplished the transition from dealing with day-to-day management matters to focusing on direction, can move through the decision-making process with speed and purpose. If a notable business coup or trading result is achieved, emotions are understandably elated with:

- A sense of team success and personal prowess.
- Surging relief.
- Growth of company standing in the market-place.
- Anticipation of rewards for self and subordinates.
- Satisfaction for owners or shareholders.

The order of priorities among these benefits may be contentious: is the motivation self-interest or successful stewardship for investors?

It is perhaps significant that these days virtually all companies with executive-only boards are private. Astute, hard-headed executives who handle the funds of major institutions are quick to seize upon a chairman whose quoted plc board neglects at least to fly its non-executive colours as a show of shareholder protection.

In private companies the pressure to introduce non-executives is slight unless heavy financial backing or personal equity stakes are involved, then nominees come into play. Outside minority shareholders are woefully short of leverage in a company which has only executive directors. An interesting situation arises when all the executive board members either are themselves owners in a buy-out, or hold equity which will shortly be exchanged for cash or valued paper on the USM – a profound equalising effect on motivations is then introduced at a stroke.

An all-executive board has the virtue of leaving no doubt as to the hands which control the issues of today and tomorrow, especially if the chief executive is also the chairman. But as companies are increasingly exposed to external scrutiny, such unquestioned, self-perpetuating power is no longer acceptable.

The combination of a decline in numbers of all-executive boards with a reduction in executive presence in unitary board concepts will undoubtedly change the influence which executives have in the direction, as against the management, of a business. This could be a retrograde step on two counts:

- UK unitary boards are already prone to retain too much control over what are really executive management decisions. To transfer the weight of executives to management committees or similar halfway houses would deny the company valuable inputs in its direction.
- Executives are conscious of their personal standing in their industry, company or community. This is enhanced when they are known to be directors, especially of a plc.

In themselves, these are not reason enough to create superfluous directorships, but in many businesses they are symptomatic of a general reluctance to delegate decision making to the executive.

One solution is wider use of two-tier boards, not dogmatically following any European pattern but rather creating a concept where one tier, the executive board, is given greater authority and where its members are also bona fide directors of the company. Such a concept is detailed towards the end of this chapter.

The non-executive board

Apart from a long-established but now rapidly changing practice in building societies, only a few banks, co-operatives and other companies exist where a board devoid of executive members finds favour – and then not among the ranks of executives. Being 'in attendance' does not have the same ring of authority, no matter how it may be dressed up.

Building societies, now comparatively unfettered in commercial terms, have been quick to introduce executives as a minority on their boards. To meet their changing status they are replacing most of their ageing traditional non-executives with a diversity of socially and commercially minded younger people.

Co-operatives face the difficulty of attempting to form a board with balanced objectivity and experience when all its directors are non-executive and also are, and represent, owners whose interests and backgrounds are in the same industry sector. Agricultural co-operatives are a case in point: grower/producers are the owners, some of whom are pressed also to act as volunteer non-executives, on a fee basis which is quite nominal.

Achieving balance is again the crucial issue. Quite apart from introducing a number of independent non-executives drawn from outside the industry, if a non-executive board is to stand a chance of performing adequately, it has to be balanced by an operational team which can and does play a major part in developing policy and strategy. In status and function that means a parallel board of executives, not a management committee. Non-executive boards which attempt to stand alone, without meaningful executive involvement in the process of direction, are unlikely to be productive. Solo boards are likely to become increasingly rare over the next ten years.

> **Comment**
> 'There is only one board, whether the directors are all non-executive or all executive.'

The parental conglomerate

In the upper echelons of board contributors there exists a group of national and international figures who direct the one hundred or so major corporations which dominate the industrial and commercial sectors in capitalist Western Europe, North America and Japan.

Executives and non-executives alike, their interests are invariably multifarious with power being exercised through a master board which controls a vast network of associate and subsidiary companies. The non-executive directors are carefully chosen through personal contacts or recommendation, can be relied upon to muster an impressive list of either national or international credentials and also have access to a broad range of established contacts.

This exclusive band is not immune either to making basic errors of judgement or, using current financial engineering techniques, to exercising the claws of a predator. Such pursuits apart, these parental conglomerates usually direct their empires in one of four ways:

- By root and branch control, following a pattern of growth and development based on long-standing business practice. Each extension of activity is meticulously planned, dovetailed into place and controlled by a central team, which views the group as a single core with related deviations.
- As merchant princedoms, a bejewelled array of unrelated companies gathered during a decade or two of judicious and opportunistic trading in, as well as through, companies. A concept in which a price tag is firmly attached to everything and everyone, it has numerous variations and practices including 'unbundling' (breaking up a conglomerate to sell off some or all of the parts in order to realise a value above the price paid for the whole). The sovereign states owe their position to gifted entrepreneurs who are possessed with vision, a remarkable sense of timing and unerring sources of information. By reputation, intelligible business philosophy and charismatic style, they galvanise the efforts of countless clones through a careful balance of operational freedoms and rigorous financial targets.
- By diversified design, a recession-proof all-weather portfolio of businesses with strong central direction and co-ordination of both strategic and financial issues. This is invariably the product of expansion-minded organisations to whom sheer size and diversity are in themselves key objectives.
- By industry-based control, now prevalent in engineering, chemicals or electronics, where a natural impetus towards manufacturing centred on a particular technology is supported by an ethos of professional management and democratic controls. Holding a loose rein, the corporate board provides liaison, guidance and judgement. In

> return it expects both effort and results but is not usually prone to summary executions in the form of sale or dismissal for short-term underperformance as may happen in a price-tagged merchant princedom.

It would be naïve to suggest that there is a single best way, since performance depends more on the collective ability of the people involved than on any particular concept. Clearly, where merchant banks and global financiers combine forces as predators on a buy and break-up spree, they are in a position to outmanoeuvre the defensive measures of all but the most adroit conglomerate boards – provided their sources of funding are not hit by nervous tremors in world economic markets. When that happens, as in 1989/90, it is the concerns which are strong in producing results through ongoing business management who hold the trump cards.

An unworldly blessing

Once in a while a breath of fresh air is felt in the still atmosphere of commercial life. The following is, I believe, such an occasion:

> **Comment**
> 'Did you say you were writing a book on business matters? Then may I commend a business venture to you – it was my uncle's, probably the most unworldly man ever known. He scorned money and simply didn't understand it, so when he told his friends he was going to run a hotel in that beauty spot in the Lebanese mountains they laughed and didn't take him seriously. But he did, and it was a great success and ran on most unusual lines.
>
> He could not suffer bores or anyone not congenial so the formula was simple: no books of any description were kept, no bills of course, and if he didn't like you he wouldn't have you, and if he liked you you couldn't

pay. And because he was a hugely popular man and there seemed to be no exchange of money, there was no tax either. He had a charming mistress who saw to it that everything ran smoothly and in cold weather that he wore wool next to his skin. She tended his narghile lovingly and well, placing the tobacco in the right state of dampness. She ran the staff who were smiling and efficient and willing at all times. His range of friends was enormous, beginning with the two muleteers who brought up the supplies from Beirut and who were so well looked after by him – or perhaps I should say Selima.

Since everyone knows that in this life vulgar money is a necessity, this was looked after by Selima. Guests would beg her – beg! – to be allowed to contribute something, which they did, but only to her. You could order any drink, any coffee and it would instantly come, without the sordid business of signing a chit. He ran his hotel strictly in a congenial manner. The good guest cooks would be singled out now and again to provide a memorable meal, so this honoured guest would choose two ladies and they would take over the kitchen for the day.

The muleteers, who could neither read nor write, would be summoned to fetch a list of provisions a yard long from Beirut and their elephantine memory was such as to never fail. And why muleteers? Simply because it was quicker than either horsedrawn cab or the Model T Ford, which needed resting after it boiled at almost every hairpin bend.'

The European-style two-tier boards

As we moved from the Model T towards the Single European Market, there is a noticeable rise in the heat of debate about both the shape and style of future boards in the United

Kingdom. Will the dreaded Vth Directive or the European Company Statute ever cross the Channel? If it was adopted in the United Kingdom, it would entail a change from the established unitary board concept to one where, as executives, company directors would be required to sit on a 'lower' tier board, with a supervisory board in a tier above. It could also mean employee directors, and would apply to all large and medium-sized companies.

Although non-executive directors are thought to perform best when in their natural habitat of a properly constituted, democratic unitary board, in the real world this ideal circumstance seldom happens. It remains the non-executive's lot either to battle away as a minority voice or to give way, and with independence a rarity the latter option often wins.

The United Kingdom's European peers now have some years' experience of the two-tier system and are pushing in the country's direction a weight of pending legislation on the subject. Having two tiers does not in itself suggest either the correctness of the principle of two-tiers or necessarily that it is a more effective way of directing a company's affairs – but both may be true.

Is is a misconception that a two-tier board necessarily means the automatic introduction of employee representation on to the so-called supervisory board. This is patently not the case. Supervisory boards were in use in Germany long before workers' representatives were appointed to them. This form of industrial democracy has to stand on its own merit and, if a company wished, could equally apply to a unitary concept.

In essence the system proposes two separate boards. First, there is a supervisory board consisting of people who do not have any executive function in the company, drawn from a variety of industrial, commercial and academic sources. They will include those who:

- Own or invest in the company.
- Provide its banking and financial services.
- Bring a balance of experience, skills and judgement to bear on matters of corporate policy.

This totally non-executive board acts within specific limits. It may not initiate policies but has the power to authorise substantial initiatives put forward by its management counterpart, such as:

- Mergers, acquisitions, disposals and joint ventures.
- Closure, transfer or fundamental change of operations.
- Financial restructuring.

The supervisory board is also responsible for the appointment or removal of members of the management board, but its supervisory function does not extend into senior management below board level. In all these respects, the scope of its members' involvement is more limited than that of its UK unitary board counterparts. Conversely, the range of interested parties represented on the supervisory board helps to create a stronger unity of purpose and commitment. This is found to increase when employee directors are appointed to represent the interests of their co-workers.

The management board is therefore left with considerable freedom and power to plan and carry out the company's business. It nevertheless needs to remain mindful of the supervisory board's existence, its broad membership and the scrutiny it will apply to any major change the management board proposes. In the event of disaster, the presence of another board with whom to share responsibility is purely cosmetic: even in these circumstances the supervisory board is not permitted to engage in the management of the company. All it can do is find another management board.

Although many UK company directors may in principle incline towards the higher American non-executive to executive ratio, they remain adamant in rejecting any moves towards the European-style two-tier formal separation of supervision and management and its associations with employee board representation.

The two key issues are the loss of the unitary board director's perceived power to rule, and the assumption that two tiers must be accompanied by mandatory employee board representation. Ironically, the directors in this instance will be likely to enjoy considerable support from trade union leaders, who also see representation as an erosive threat to their power. They may remember the story of the two dogs who spent every day snapping and snarling at each other from either side of a fence – take the fence away and with it may go their *raison d'être*.

The North American boards

Although basically unitary, board composition in the United States is heavily weighted in favour of the non-executive as a means of providing wise counsel for the chief executive, whose operating officers (vice-presidents) are kept quite separate. US practice is increasingly being accepted by UK companies.

First there is a corporate board of ten to thirteen directors, of whom only two or three are executive; they include the chief executive and the finance director. The remaining seven to ten members are all non-executive, mostly senior people drawn from unrelated businesses, government administration or professional practice. The legal burden which now bears down on US companies almost guarantees that one seat is reserved for a lawyer, who, apart from having a disciplined mind, has the legal experience to help the board appreciate the implications of law and interpret the advice of their professional lawyers.

The US-style board not only monitors executive operational performance, but its non-executive directors also wield considerable power and influence in the making of policy decisions and, more recently, act as final adjudicators in highly leveraged management buy-outs. Additionally, these non-executives are also under considerable personal pressure to perform through the risks they run of shareholder negligence suits.

Secondly, there is an executive board which runs the company and in turn is run by the chief executive or president. It is a team of personally motivated, results-oriented people whose standing within and without the corporation is a close match to that of the corporate directors. They enjoy salaries, stock options and performance-related payments as substantial as one might expect in a highly charged capitalist society.

The status and prestige accorded to executives in the United States clearly demonstrates their importance in both company and community alike. Typically, they also introduce flamboyant titles. The 'Senior Executive Vice-President Corporate Marketing' is an interesting contrast to the UK equivalent, who may also not happen to be on the corporate board and accordingly is 'a member of the Management Committee'. No wonder the status-starved businessmen of the United Kingdom cling desperately to any position which carries the élite title of 'Director'.

The Japanese board

Meanwhile the Japanese scene presents a stark contrast, described in the following way by Shoichi Saba, who is also a non-executive director of ICI:

> In Japan hitherto, the boards of big companies have consisted of internal appointees and outside directors, usually members of a main bank, institutional shareholders, or associated companies. The chief practical difference is that our boards are invariably far larger. Against ICI's 16 main board directors, for example, Toshiba has as many as 28, and Mitsui and Nissan up to 49 and 44 respectively.
>
> The ICI meeting I attended today took three hours. In Japan, most board meetings last from half an hour to an hour: the meetings tend to be formal events for final approvals and decisions. Key decisions are also taken at executive officers' meetings or executive committees.

This is indicative of the degree of decentralised decision making which exists in Japanese organisations. The almost indecently brief meetings may suggest a purely ceremonial occasion but this is far from the case: they not only signify a binding commitment by all who attend, but also put a seal on agreements and decisions made collectively down the management line.

UK BOARDS: THE SINGLE EUROPEAN MARKET AND BEYOND

Common sense dictates that UK boards will eventually move towards some form of two-tier arrangement, warts and all, and in practice many companies are already taking that route. It is arguable that in the majority of instances the unitary concept has not worked to a company's advantage in that its usual composition and style makes it prone to an imbalance of power, a debilitating clutter of unsuitable or inept members, constraints on executives and restrictive practices which lead to the promotion of self-interest. As long as the present UK unitary system remains open to abuse, and continues to be abused, pressure to introduce a mandatory two-tier alternative will continue to grow. Such pressure may stem from financial institutions, regulatory bodies or EC legislation.

Creating two boards is in itself no cure-all, but a number of features inherent in the system seem to merit the transition. Briefly they are designed to:

- Identify clearly the different function of each board.
- Separate the chairman and chief executive roles.
- Increase use of part-time chairmen who are skilled in co-ordinating governance of policy rather than executive issues.
- Reduce the likelihood of decisions being 'engineered' or 'powered' through a meeting against consensus, or of the self-interest of particular directors prejudicing the exercise of due care and diligence.
- Give greater independence or room for manoeuvre to the chief executive and the team, and recognition of the executive director's position at the top of the management pyramid.
- Sharpen the focus of the independent non-executives on their policy- and performance-monitoring role without restraining creative liaison between non-executives and executives.
- Provide an opportunity for effective representation of shareholders or financial institutions, and in small

companies family or founder ownership, without their interference in operational matters.

- Lessen the influence of City short-termist factions over some plc unitary boards, where the former play almost an upper-tier or dominant policy-making role.
- Provide a forum which may be used for the introduction of employees as non-executive representative directors whose primary role is to express the interests of employees.

Co-ordinating the function of two boards is not an insuperable problem provided an overall concept is understood and the suggested format matches need. UK companies have devised and lived with a fair share of highly intricate board structures for a century or more. Now is not the time blindly to copy others or, under threat, to be panicked into action; but nor is it the time for putting heads in sand and hoping that the problems will go away.

THE UK TWIN-BOARD CONCEPT

After all the bitter protestations and arguments are spent, negotiation and compromise will doubtless result in a unique Anglo-Saxon blend, hopefully including Celtic overtones. The United Kingdom need not follow its European counterparts in either application or terminology. For example:

- Use of the term 'two-tier' immediately suggests inequality between the two boards. In practice, each has to have an equal presence, responsibility and parallel orientation with the other, rather like twins.
- In a similar way, preference might be given to 'executive' board rather than 'management' board, to 'policy' rather than 'supervisory'.
- Noting progressive changes already made in some UK companies, linking directors can be introduced to counteract a real sense of remoteness often experienced in European companies, where the board of each tier operates in almost total isolation.

The UK system may be something like this:

1. The overall responsibility for the direction of a company rests with its directors, who include executives and non-executives, presided over by a part-time chairman – in a way similar to many current unitary boards. However, in this system the directors (except the Chief Executive and Financial Director) chiefly carry out their duties as members of either an executive board or a policy board. It is not difficult to divide the various functions of the two boards when following the general principles that:

(a) an executive board initiates and actions;
(b) a policy board advises, approves and monitors.

2. Each board normally operates independently except on perhaps three or four occasions a year when all the directors come together in joint meeting under the chairmanship of the policy board chairman. These meetings are used to ratify proposals which may fundamentally change either the nature or purpose of the business, or which finalise their joint commitment to key policy, strategy and business plans, budget approvals, interim statements, year-end results and the recommendation of dividend payments.

3. The executive board is chaired by the chief executive, meets weekly or monthly as required, and its members are all executive. That is, in medium or large groups, they are likely to be functional directors with such responsibilities as finance, technology or group services – plus the managing directors of subsidiary or divisional companies. In smaller companies, they could be directors who head finance, marketing, manufacturing, technical development or similar operations.

The executive board is given wider sole authority and decision-making powers over expenditure, development and operations than is usual in current experience. Its primary functions are to:

(a) run the business in line with agreed objectives;
(b) initiate and propose, or recast, company objectives, policies, strategies, business plans and budgets;

(c) propose changes in the nature or purpose of the business.

In the latter two points the executive board refers to the policy board for authorisation, items of major significance then being matters for a joint meeting and, possibly, shareholder approval.

4. The policy board is chaired by a part-time chairman whose prior relationship with the business might have been as an executive but who is normally an independent, recruited on merit from outside the company. Meeting, say, six to eight times a year, its members, apart from the chief executive and finance director, must include at least two non-executives who are genuinely independent. It may also have an equivalent, but not greater, number of non-executives who are nominee representatives of either external parties with a direct interest in the company or, if policy, of employees.

The function of the policy board combines being supportive of the executive, creative when assessing proposals, and objective when monitoring executive performance and results of activities under their control. In addition to considering and approving or referring back the executive board's blueprint for development, it receives budget or profit plans and regular operational and financial reports. It is also required to:

(a) elect a chairman and nominate the chief executive, specify their authorities and, if necessary, remove and replace the chairman or, through the chairman, the chief executive;
(b) through committees, on which either the chief executive or finance director sit, approve the hiring, firing and succession plans for senior management, recommend a top salary structure and performance related payments schemes, and carry out periodic information and financial audit.

5. In contrast to no-link practice in European two-tier systems, the chief executive and the finance director sit

on both boards and provide a basis for their close liaison. This crucial linking process also provides a regular opportunity for the non-executives to work face-to-face with the company's leading executives both at meetings of the policy board and at informal sessions or board committees.

6. Members of the twin boards, being bona fide directors of the company, should be fully described in the annual report, company returns, prospectus or other relevant published information and, as directors, assume all the duties, responsibilities and liabilities of that role under company legislation.

7. This twin-board arrangement would be applicable to all listed plcs and private companies where substantial shareholding is outside the control of directors. It could, of course, equally apply to any private company which preferred that approach in the direction of its business, but in practice it is perhaps best suited to those with an annual turnover above £5 million.

8. In total the number of directors involved in a twin-board system will vary but, except in quite small companies, less than seven might be unusual. The seven represented by (the chief executive and finance director on both boards) + (a policy board with chairman plus two non-executives) + (an executive board having two executives other than the chief executive and financial director). There is no maximum, but the figure is governed by the complement of either executives or independent non-executives. In total, the proposals are unlikely to result in any significant upward change against a current average of eight to nine directors; it is their arrangement which is important.

CONCLUSION

It would be nonsense to suggest that unitary boards cannot be effective. Many patently are and perform with excellence; these would have little difficulty in changing to a twin-board system even though little direct benefit might be gained. The majority of boards, however, are less accomplished in either their performance or their self-regulation in the light of society's current expectations. For many directors, executive and non-executive alike, the adjustments demanded in transition could be painful.

Leaving aside the question of employee representation, the dual hurdles of policy board monitoring and proper demarcation of executive status have sooner or later to be cleared in both letter and spirit. Whatever the route, imposition or natural evolution, the non-executive's influence in board affairs will continue to grow.

8

Nominees

Like numerous chairmen I find a nominee's position in the boardroom scene to be an ever-taxing conundrum. The very term 'nominee' conjures up chessboard rather than main-board images. The generally accepted definition, however, is less emotive. It describes the role as that of a director who is appointed by, or at the instigation of, any party with a substantial interest in the company.

The interpretation of the word 'interest' is crucial. It may indicate either a degree of curiosity or a substantial right, share or claim. Standing alone it is a nebulous term unless it carries a qualifying prefix to denote whether the interest is specific or general, and for oneself or on behalf of others not mentioned.

At the inception of the joint-stock company, shareholders held the view that the composition of their board was very much in their common or general interest. The subsequent years have seen an evolution in board power towards its self-perpetuation, with publicly quoted companies owned only nominally by shareholders whose decline in numbers is matched by a decline in the level of interest and attention they are prepared, or encouraged, to give to the company.

REPRESENTATIVE NOMINEES

Investing institutions and financial houses, which between them command almost three-quarters of all shareholding, have only recently begun to step up their pressure on chairmen to produce what might be termed 'a balanced board'. They profess to place great store upon a chairman's ability to mould the co-directors into a team which shares the same interests and objectives. However, they studiously avoid emphasising the term 'independent' as a prefix to the non-executive title – understandably perhaps, as its definition may well preclude them from putting forward their own favoured candidate.

A director's representative duty, as we have seen, is to the company – to all the shareholders, present and future. That specifically excludes any sectional interest or the use of privileged information, indeed any information which is not equally available to all. What a director needs to know, and has a right to know in order to function, is not common knowledge and may only be told to others in the bona fide interests of the company.

A nominee should automatically be *persona non grata* if the primary motive of the nominator, and by implication the nominee, is to safeguard specific interests to the exclusion of others. This makes for debilitating boardroom intrigue and power play; indeed, were it not for the decorative charm of a nominee's leverage many nominees' directors would not continue to be there.

So what is the position of a nominee who joins the board at the behest or 'suggestion' of a major shareholder, investing institution or financial house – and how do chairmen and their board colleagues react to such a proposal? This forced choice method of making an appointment is a tortuous path which in itself seldom produces a satisfactory result for either company or owners. Its very nature must raise doubts as to the nominee's independence. Might the nominee be there in preparation for a subtle seizure of control? Does the nominee act in a similar capacity in a number of companies, and if so to whom lies the nominee's true allegiance?

The burden of the representative nominee is as unfair to the individual as it is to the company. No matter how cognisant of the company's general well-being are the views they express, representative nominees will seldom be perceived as truly independent. And sponsors themselves are not excluded from the damaging repercussions of failure. More than a few battered venture-capital companies have privately voiced their dismay and surprise at shifts in policy, changes in direction, unexpected downturns in trading results or near disasters which appear to happen in spite of the presence of their nominee.

> **Comment**
> When reviewing a less than creditable board performance, its chairman commented: 'We don't run anything of importance through the board, not with those two bastards [nominees, I believe] listening in. It's just rubber stamping – the real business is dealt with by the executive committee a week earlier.'

In spite of the widespread use of nominees, leaders in the City or in business institutions representing either companies or directors are quick to sit astride the fence when faced with the propriety of the nominee issue and to declare neither positive support nor outright rejection of the practice. Such silence leads one to suspect that they feel somewhat awkward about a nominee's legal position in the pursuit of sectional interests when a conflict of loyalties may arise – but condemn they do not.

Occasionally a voice is heard. For example the Institute of Directors 'deprecates' such appointments by particular financial bodies as being inconsistent with a director's duty. Going further, it suggests possible change in a company's Articles to obviate or otherwise restrict the nominee role. PRO NED takes a softer line, considering the use of nominees a 'disadvantage'. Others emit only a convenient hush and pretend it does not happen.

> **Comment**
> 'The majority of non-executive directors in companies of less than £10 million turnover appear to be nominees for financial institutions who seek to serve two masters. Although their first line of responsibility is to the company, from a practical point of

> view their continued survival in office is more likely to depend on being closer to the institution.'

Shareholders should have the right to tell their chairman to take action if they believe the board is in any way inadequate; indeed, they should be positively encouraged to do so. Institutions and banks, who own most shares anyway, are ideally placed and have the muscle to take such steps. However, the application of pressure or leverage to force acceptance of a nominated representative is quite wrong – and probably illegal as it verges on requiring the representative to act unlawfully.

INVESTING NOMINEES

Investing nominees are at best a commercial hazard through which a course may with difficulty be steered; at worst, their presence denotes a deliberate act of sheer piracy.

The changing shape of the UK economy and the stimulated spawning of new enterprises have in turn encouraged the development of a number of small, private financial services groups which specialise in providing techniques and resources to restructure ailing company finances or deal with disasters, or both. They simply look for investment potential among businesses which have a sound base but, for a multitude of reasons, are temporarily in trouble. The precise depth and duration of the trouble is usually not altogether clear to the owners and directors.

Small companies should not conclude that this phenomenon is peculiar to them, for it is a route well trodden by those looking for a means of gaining control of much larger enterprises.

Not knowing the answers, which way to turn or how to survive is just as much a peril for the established business as for the new. Therein lies their dilemma and the *raison d'être* of many an opportunist predator.

The likely counselling and remedial health treatment which follows will include 'in-depth' analysis, optional diets of relative discomfort, a low ebb of threatened desertion and pointers toward survival – subject, of course, to certain conditions. Three elements will invariably appear in the package of the 'adviser':

- Provision of financial services with appropriate charges.
- Forfeiture of part shareholding.
- Board representation – one or two seats, or the chair.

Some owners learn quickly as they are led to the brink of relinquishing control, then choose to ignore their advisers and regardless of perils battle on alone. In later years they are perhaps able to reflect upon those eventful times, the lessons learned and the not entirely unhelpful advice which came their way. Others, low in confidence, feel it unwise to ignore any offer of a helping hand, even if strings are attached, because the alternative might be terminal. But once they are committed, activity intensifies in relation to both the board role and the direction of change, and it soon becomes evident that the new appointees see their role as anything but non-executive.

It is not just the individual persuasive power wielded by these 'nominees' which must be taken into account, but the combined leverage of money supply, an equity stake and imposed executive control. Quite often businesses seem to melt away from the grasp of their original owners, or the owners are left with a minority stake and virtually no say in the running of a business merged into a fashionable mini-conglomerate or bolted on to some solid core structure.

Nominees are losing credibility as demand for the identification of their role increases but fails to be met within normal unitary board reporting. In two-tier or twin board concepts their purpose and contribution is specifically targeted to the respective supervisory or policy board where any notions they have to apply undue weight can be readily curtailed. However, until differences are resolved as to which board concept will predominate, the potentially debilitating effect of nominees remains a matter for concern.

An effective method of dealing with the nominee question involves acceptance of only three principles:

- It is a chairman's task to staff the board with a suitable mix of people, including non-executives. The chairman should receive and deal with suggestions for appointments to the board and is responsible for guiding co-directors in deciding who, why and when.
- Unless promoters of nominees have more than fifty per cent of the votes, are determined to have their own way, or are bloody-minded enough to undermine the chairman, they should change practice: make known any criticisms of the board, then leave the chairman to do the job. If necessary, they can ask to be told of candidates at the penultimate appointment stage and express their support or disapproval, the chairman remaining final arbiter.
- As and when a nominee is appointed, the subsequent company Report and Accounts should show each nominee's credentials (as it should for all non-executives) and also disclose the nominator's identity.

None of these proposals precludes erstwhile promoters or nominators from helping the chairman by throwing the hats of people they consider suitable into the ring. Many do so already and to good effect, or steer chairmen towards a central agency such as the Institute of Director's Appointments Service or PRO NED.

CONCLUSION

It may take years before there is a significant shift in the balance between the current minority of independent non-executives and those who represent either their own interests or the interests of a sectional power. Not everyone even accepts that such a situation exists and they will understandably protest in strident terms against any suggestion to the contrary. Averages take little account of individual cases and in many companies where all non-executive directors are independent such an imbalance of pressures plainly does not arise.

The standing of non-executives has through the years been tarnished by evidence of bias, ineptitude, patronage and covert representation. The image is changing favourably through wider knowledge of the role and a concerted clean-up campaign. Realistically, one must accept that in business life one person's folly makes another's opportunity, but it is a grave misjudgement even to think twice about trying to preserve nominees as an endangered species.

9

The Non-Executive Role in Mergers and Acquisitions

Pundits from time to time claim that the freedom of the market-place or the rationale of market forces relates in some way to exercising egalitarian principles. In practice, entering the market is akin to moving one's habitat into the middle of a jungle; to conceive it as the Garden of Eden is both naïve and foolhardy.

Not surprisingly, there is high demand for experienced non-executives who can give sound, impartial advice to executive colleagues regarding transactions with potentially large financial implications for themselves or the fortunes of their company. During the past few years the demand has intensified, and for three main reasons:

- The impetus for realignment of control within key international industries based in the United States, Europe and Japan continues unabated into the 1990s.
- Groups of companies find it easier to change the portfolio of their businesses than to take on board the problems of sustaining a multi-product formation. In the process they are attracted to the potential bottom-line benefits of buying, breaking apart and selling companies simply as a trading exercise.
- Communications technology now gives twenty-four-hour interlinking between the burgeoning centres of global financial services, and has opened the door to innovative deal makers who use their skills to write a new set of rules for the merger, acquisition and divestment game.

As a result of these developments, the boards of predators and targets alike are faced with a series of new complexities. Access to good advisers may solve some problems, but ultimately a board must decide on a course of action for which it alone is responsible. On such occasions it can be worth a king's ransom to have one or two non-executives experienced in the craft of corporate policy decision-making and who can play a leading part in formulating a sound acquisition or defence strategy.

Directors, especially non-executive directors, of all but the smallest companies need to be well versed in the diversity of spin-off implications from even the most commonplace merger or acquisition activities. From the moment a bid lands on the table life will never be quite the same again. Pick up a copy of the *Financial Times* on almost any day and note the variety of mergers, acquisitions or divestments which are featured. The large number only illustrates the perpetual build and break-up cycle, now accepted as commonplace when high-tension trading markets are operating.

Mergers, properly defined, are very rare in the United Kingdom and, by definition, have to be agreed. The merger is usually a fairly orderly and confidential affair provided it moves quickly past the point of no return. The two company boards have debated reasons, done their sums and made conclusive recommendations to their respective shareholders. However, if a third party steps in, a quite different and possibly acrimonious situation may arise. Similarly, a hostile bid can be the signal for the immediate drawing-up of battle lines and support forces. In both cases non-executive involvement is crucial.

ANYTHING GOES!

In sheer scale and audacity there are few commercial events to match the spate of merger and acquisition activity which erupted in the late 1980s. The opportunities of an over-indulgent if not naïve regulatory environment, coupled with a computer-linked market-place on both sides of the

Atlantic, were seized upon by a circle of internationally minded entrepreneurs. In this they enlisted the support of an aggressive breed of bankers and brokers, who from eyries in Wall Street and the City mastermind moves on the corporate chessboard and with flair introduce a variety of novel company restructuring and funding techniques under the well chosen banner of financial engineering.

A merchant bank's traditional function of providing its client company with sound advice on financial development has now been replaced by that of exerting significant influence over a number of players in the acquisition game, if not in fact becoming a player in its own right. With the exception of top international establishments such as Lazard Freres, 'anything goes' is the music of the day and little is looked on as shocking. Competition in personal prowess runs high. In efforts to forage for new business it has not been unknown for a bank to approach a non-client company, propose that it should make a takeover bid, identify a suggested target, then produce a well-engineered formula to raise the necessary finance and lines of credit. In these circumstances it might be reasonable to ask who is calling the tune, and in whose best interests.

Hostile bids can represent a definitive means of arriving at true share value. They may, in fact, be seen as hostile only by the directors of the target company, who may be opposed more for personal than for business reasons. Directors cannot, however, ignore the value gap which a bid reveals and in a matter of days they usually counter with forecasts of increased profits and dividends. Stockholders are often told by their directors to reject an offer even when it carries a premium over the pre-bid price. In the United States, directors of Time favoured a merger with Warner against a bid from Paramount; they ignored the wishes of a shareholding majority and a court upheld that decision.

Whether or not the reasons to oppose are justifiable, a hostile approach has an air of drama for participants and onlookers alike as a each side's gladiator enters the arena, while in the wings wait some of the less savoury performers. In this context, corporate raiders, arbitrageurs, insider deals and mezzanine finance scarcely raise an eyebrow. And not all acquisitions are so well publicised. There have been, and still are, a string of potential dealers who operate from less exposed positions.

NORTH AMERICAN MEGABIDS

To help curb the excesses of dubious bid practices, corporations in the United States have used to good effect the dominant number of independent non-executive directors on their boards. In a predatory company, such non-executives acting in concert can provide an unbiased check on proposed bid terms. In defensive situations, their role as fair-minded arbitrators allows them to recommend which amongst several bids appears best for stockholders – especially if one is a leveraged buy-out proposed by the executives seeking to have financial control of the business they manage. Not surprisingly, the pressures applied to non-executives, either directly or indirectly, reflect the enormous sums involved – it is no time to be guileless or faint-hearted.

The dramatic battle for RJR Nabisco is a useful case study. When eventually a decision had to be made between a management buy-out and Kohlberg Kravis Roberts, a New York firm of specialists in debt-financed takeovers or leveraged buy-outs, it was Nabisco chairman Charles Hugel and his non-executive directors who had the ultimate say as to winner and terms. This was no mean responsibility when the final consideration was in the order of $25 billion and bidding began at $17.6 billion. The last somewhat ironical twist in this biggest ever business deal was that the non-executives decided against their former executive colleagues, even though theirs was the higher bid. Fees to banking and financial services amounted to a reported $700 million, with total costs to the new corporate owners rising to a staggering $1 billion.

Within five years the rush of leveraged buy-outs or debt-financed takeovers in the United States has led to one-tenth, or over $400 billion, of equity in non-financial companies being replaced by debt – a pace so hectic that John Creedon, president of MetLife the giant investor, was prompted to say 'Larger and more complicated transactions and mega-deals pose real threats to the integrity of the capital markets in this country.'

Some idea of the scale of business was shown when Drexel Burnham Lambert (DBL), a fiercely aggressive Wall Street investment bank and dealer in high-yield junk bonds, agreed in 1989 to pay a fine of $650 million to the US law-enforcement authorities for security law transgressions. A gigantic sum, it is perhaps put into perspective by the fact that DBL's former head of junk bond operations, Michael Milken, in one year had reportedly been paid over $500 million and was shortly to face charges of securities fraud for which fines could eventually total over $1 billion.

In the United States, leveraged buy-outs peaked with Nabisco. Now the practice is not only less acceptable, but the vulnerability of associated high gearing has been savagely exposed in times of static markets.

THE UNITED KINGDOM: A BUSTLING SCENE

Meanwhile UK companies enjoyed a series of victories in their corporate assault on North America, which in 1988 produced more than three hundred mergers or acquisitions valued in excess of $14 billion – a ratio of ten to one over bids in the reverse direction.

Within the United Kingdom, activity reached an equally frenetic peak with more recorded mergers and acquisitions than in all the remaining EC countries put together. Each day the media featured another variation in a stream of buy-outs, buy-ins, earn-outs, cram-downs and other novel acquisition practices.

On the face of it, to concentrate on mergers and acquisitions to this degree in a book about non-executives might seem irrelevant – it is far from being the case. To be of value to a board each non-executive has to be aware not only of changes in power or ownership within a company's market sector with the resulting threats or opportunities, but also be able to evaluate the techniques used both in attack and defence. A majority of non-executives will at some time be on the board of a company involved in this sort of activity – it is too late waiting until the day, co-directors will be rightly unimpressed.

To pre-empt the effects of static economies and in advance of 1992 many companies are following the lead of Lord Weinstock's GEC, Arthur Walsh's STC or SmithKline Beecham in realigning cross-border industry partnerships to consolidate their position in the European and US markets. Occasionally the City is jolted into a higher gear as, for instance, when Hanson plc secured its bid for Consolidated Gold Fields, or Sir James Goldsmith, having studied the corporate gyrations in North America, decided the time was right to apply leveraged buy-out techniques in the United Kingdom and launched his own debt-financed bid to 'unbundle' the seemingly impregnable BAT conglomerate.

Although BAT might have been considered dull by market makers, it did not have terminal symptoms. Nor did it deserve the generally prescribed cure for sluggishly performing UK companies, or those inflicted with inept management – a cure simple in the extreme – to be taken over by others who profess to offer greater competence and skill in the use of assets.

Skill in using assets is a crucial factor, and the track record of a predator usually determines the degree of financial support available. This was not the case, however, when a nervous market prompted institutional investors to withdraw support from a sound and well-managed DRG and consign it to the breakers' yard.

In spirited markets, buy-in or buy-out managements need nothing more than a shelf company as a corporate vehicle to couple to a high-profile team of financial manipulators. The difficulty is raising enough finance, based on the target's assets, while simultaneously keeping the support of shareholders and investors as the debt to equity ratio goes through the roof. Buying a company with its own money and servicing its bridging loan from a squeezed cash flow sounds simple, but there is trouble ahead if the market suddenly becomes listless.

Seeing all this corporate financial wizardry at work, one wonders if great and lasting benefits result from acquisitions, and if so to whom they accrue. The practice is less evident in Germany or Japan and neither country seems to have suffered economic traumas as a result – in fact quite the opposite. German companies, with cash reserves strong enough to meet strategic investments, enjoy considerable independence from external pressures because of long-term relationships with their bankers who are frequently represented on company supervisory boards, and it is not thought fashionable to trade companies as an alternative to commodities. A unified Germany will not be slow to benefit from this arrangement.

With the advent of the Single Market, Europe could provide an astonishing array of new targets to test the ingenuity and combative strength of Anglo-American bankers and industrial leaders. But the nature of the equity of many continental companies makes hostile bids more difficult and EC Commissioners are likely to use all available powers to frustrate the performance of high-wire acts in major financing deals. That is quite apart from the economic complications which arise from an enlarged market on Europe's eastern borders.

TRADING IN COMPANIES

It is now quite commonplace for a subsidiary company to have three or more different owners within a decade, each buyer having its own plan to strip off, convert or bolt on various bits and pieces to add value on subsequent disposal. Selling a company just to improve the appearance of its parent's balance sheet might be a clever exercise on paper, and company trading may excite executives keen to build both reputation and personal fortune, but a board's remit should never be so narrowly focused. Non-executive directors have to keep their ethical hats firmly in place and assess whether the short-term interests of a small number of opportunist shareholders are more important than the cumulative effect that enforced changes may have on employees and the business.

Leveraged buy-outs apart, dramatic deals are generally outside the scope of smaller companies, although few escape their commercial repercussions. It would be unnatural if small companies failed also to look for a share in the action and to explore the range of mergers and acquisitions open to them.

CONCEPTS FOR THE SMALLER COMPANY

A different approach is made by some venture-capital companies including 3i, a long-standing industry investor. One of their imaginative concepts for growth is directed towards the owners of established private companies who, unsure of the future, are anxious to realise some reward for their past labours. In the plan, they are invited to transfer management control and part equity into the hands of paid professional executives who, although not housed in their stables, are vetted by 3i and are guaranteed financial backing.

Arrangements of this nature are apt to spawn some quite unusual board compositions. Apart from appointing executives a new investor finds comfort in having its own non-executive nominees in place, whilst the original owners also expect to retain watchdog seats. As a result the board has non-executives who are representatives and in no way independent. Its new life begins like a cosy joint venture, but as each additional tranche of capital is injected the balance of power inevitably swings away from the original founders.

In another vein, sunrise enterprises with ebullient, capital-hungry managements face a market-place awash with ready money and over one hundred venture-capital groups at which to aim. Nevertheless, they still need board credibility to support management and its business plan. Venture-capital groups have had mixed fortunes in succouring new businesses and now take the view that a seasoned part-time chairman plus two genuinely independent non-executive directors are a prerequisite to their involvement.

SAFEGUARDING INTERESTS

Shareholders and investors expect the independent non-executives to safeguard their interests if their company is involved in a merger or acquisition. Although company law and tighter Stock Exchange rules now impose more stringent disciplines on the scope and accuracy of published information, it is still the board's duty to ensure that such requirements are fully met. Non-executives must be satisfied that the company's position is clearly presented, and those who have taken part in a stringent verification process will appreciate the way in which supporting information should be examined when drawing up a prospectus.

Non-executives who combine this experience with that of corporate decision making in predatory and defensive activities, and who have more than a passing acquaintance with financial engineering techniques, are understandably highly sought after. Their value lies in their ability to:

- Distil out the commercial logic and relate that to the company's broader strategic plans.
- Give sound creative suggestions to improve proposed action plans.
- Help guide the board through the minefields of the City's square mile.
- Keep the interests of employees, suppliers and society in proper balance with those of shareholders or investors.
- Take an independent and objective stance if other members of the board or management are personally involved.

One well-documented instance of non-executive contribution in a buy-out was at Haden. Philip Ling explains:

> I joined Haden plc as managing director in September 1984, at which time the company was valued on the stock market at about £20 million. Four months later we were on

the receiving end of a hostile takeover bid from Trafalgar House plc which valued the business at £37 million.

The board of directors vigorously resisted that takeover attempt as we believed that the price offered was far too low and that Haden would not fit well with Trafalgar. In the end, as a defence against Trafalgar, the Haden executive directors formed their own company and raised £60 million and made a rival offer for Haden plc.

This offer could only proceed if it was recommended to Haden shareholders by the board of Haden and by Schroder Wagg, Haden's merchant bankers. But the executive directors of Haden could not participate in this because they were now fully committed to the new bidding company.

Consequently it fell to the Haden non-executives to consider the offer. Indeed the non-executives ended up negotiating with the executives to establish the fullest possible price for Haden. Like many takeover transactions the negotiations were completed at 4 a.m. in the morning and the agreed deal announced to the Stock Exchange as the market opened that day.

The deal went through to everybody's satisfaction. The Haden shareholders obtained £60 million cash which was considered a very full price and was three times higher than the business had been valued at a few months earlier. The executive directors retained their independence and obtained important shareholdings in the buy-out company which was renamed Haden Group. Some two years later Haden Group was merged with P & W MacLellan plc, and the combined company named Haden MacLellan Holdings plc is listed on the London stock market.

Without the crucial and delicate role played by the Haden non-executives, the buy-out of the public company would not have been possible. They ensured that the executive directors, who were seeking to buy the Haden business, not only paid the highest price they could afford but also a price which was full and fair to Haden shareholders.

A merger situation of quite different complexion led to this comment from a non-executive who was less than happy with his experience:

> Within a few days of the announcement all directors were invited to meet late one evening with a Mr — who, as far as I can remember, was with a City firm of accountants. A notable figure, he was not an official adviser to the company, but it was said he had a reputation for mounting resistance to takeovers. After the relevant meeting I commented that he had, from the outset, assumed resistance; he had not objectively set out the pros and cons of merger.
>
> As the weeks passed I came to the conclusion that, for many reasons, the merger was desirable. At the crucial board meeting I was alone in favouring acceptance of the bid – the bid failed.
>
> Subsequently, complaints were made about the questions I asked and pressure was put on me to resign. I refused and instead did not submit my name for re-election at the next AGM.

Records indicate that only half of all mergers and acquisitions seem to achieve their intended results, and by that token half fail. While this 'corporate roller-coaster' may express the free working of market forces in a capitalist society and provides an exhilarating ride for those aboard, one suspects the principal beneficiaries are the fee collectors who help the optimistic to climb on board – and the disillusioned to stagger off!

GOING PRIVATE

In spite of earnest public relations efforts by both CBI and City spokesmen, their paper is just not thick enough to cover the cracks which separate the aims of people who direct a business from the aims of those who trade in the value of its equity. Non-executives need to be aware of who is calling the tune in determining policy – is it the board or some unseen figures in the City?

It is arguable that short-termist investors, dubious techniques used in arbitrage or corporate raiding and lapses in performance by some prominent members of the banking and institutional fraternity have combined to reduce severely the level of confidence in current Stock Exchange practice – to the degree that many quoted companies are opting to privatise and return to a path of self-determination. Once the immediate financial benefits of going to market have been absorbed, the original owners also frequently find unacceptable the change in their status to that of salaried professional manager. Moreover, the trend towards privatisation is further accelerated by a favourable although increasingly cautious market attitude to the viability of management buy-outs. Ironically, these often have short-termist objectives themselves, with new owners having in mind a substantial profit on their investment when they return the company to market in two or three years.

In theory, a change from public to private should not alter a non-executive's role but in practice it does. 'Going private' clearly implies that the owners intend to exercise a greater degree of control, pursue their own short- or long-term views, not be answerable to anyone except themselves and have a strong enough board presence comfortably to quell opposition should it ever arise.

Comment
'In a large private company, there are two types of non-executive director – the major family shareholder and the outside director. This is a situation where the non-executive director has some difficulty playing his role because the shareholding non-executives quite naturally believe they are best able to protect their own interests and expect the executives to run the business.'

This creation of two distinct types of non-executive is not unique and is found even in many plcs where family domination persists. Without independence the outside director's role becomes somewhat superfluous; with it the task is still exacting.

CONCLUSION

Within the boardroom, the value of having someone with plc and mergers and acquisitions experience among the non-executive directors is becoming increasingly evident. The practice of trading in companies requires a nucleus of independently minded non-executives who are sensitive to the implications of a predator's advances and can temper the more extravagant acquisitive ambitions of their executive colleagues. In the coming years these factors will largely determine how UK companies continue to develop in North America and establish themselves in a European market which may be almost double its present size.

10

Part-Time Executive Roles – a Non-Executive's Option

During the UK recession of the early and mid-1980s, everyone concerned with business witnessed a storm of events which forced thousands of executives, at all stages in the management pyramid, to face the prospect of a sudden and irrevocable change in their assumed career scenarios. It resulted in a surge of voluntary interest in the non-executive role and had a profound and lasting effect upon the attitude of executives towards part-time working.

Executives who have a mainstream or full-time position with one company clearly shows their singular career interest. In contrast it is difficult to identify the primary intention of those who spread their activities over a variety of separate and unrelated businesses, especially if they do not necessarily carry out a similar function in each. They may be non-executives in one company, project executives in another, perhaps nominees or investment directors in a third and additionally be available for other work through one of the burgeoning executive stand-by agencies. The common denominator, of course, is that none of these positions is full time, although together they may more than fill each week.

The fact that thousands of executives now find considerable satisfaction in this mode of working is itself quite remarkable because until a few years ago the practice of part-time employment, though well known, was seldom associated with senior businessmen and women. It was thought equally unlikely that anyone in orthodox mid-career, and enjoying success, might contemplate switching direction into a 'plural' activity. It happens now and, although the initiatives which brought the change about were anything but voluntary, this flexible method of providing management and board resources looks set to become a permanent feature of company life.

THE SHAKE-OUT

Much has already been written about the long-standing causes for recession and especially about the directors and executives who failed to plan, innovate or manage change or who choked their businesses to death with outdated attitudes and outmoded practices.

The effects were savage and less predictable. Shoals of senior managers who were previously shielded now found themselves included in the inevitable cutbacks and closures. Businesses and sometimes whole industries disappeared and with them the security of a lifetime in management. A much-vaunted measure of ability amongst executives who survived was their capacity to cut the head-count and take whole layers out of the management cake.

Opportunities to move back into the mainstream dissolved like a mirage as traditional pensionable ages plunged or were replaced by an exit method called 'taking early retirement', which could be applied to anyone over fifty. The executive market-place flooded with people who, in monetary terms, were generally not too close to the poverty line. Most companies were fair and some generous in their settlements; indeed, in such situations it was the concept of a caring company which inspired the development of a now blossoming outplacement industry.

OPTIONS

For the displaced executive it became a question of choosing between taking absolute retirement, playing a more remote role or returning to a full-time career. In the latter case executives faced three options:

- To pitch back in the mainstream, wherever, whenever and however, as the only means of personal satisfaction and financial survival.
- To have a variety of jobs all associated with the activities of a company board, for example combining the roles of part-time chairman, part-time executive director and one or more non-executive directorships, all with different companies, but all concerned with their experience in company direction.
- To leave behind the single company concept and put their accumulated executive skills on temporary hire.

Opportunities were there to be taken as business leaders fought to revive in management a will and determination to manage the transition from chaos to a new enterprise philosophy.

BACK IN THE MAINSTREAM

With hindsight, many see the effects of the recession as a happy release or a blessing in disguise. Executives, now freed from mental constraints and old-fashioned systems, were understandably eager to bring their sharpened talents to bear, full time, on the interests of another company.

Out of the turbulent recession was born a belief among strategists that the way ahead lay in an extensive reshaping of company portfolios, and it became fashionable to shed businesses which no longer fitted into 'core' activities. This, coupled with growth in service industries and a better appreciation of the niche market, opened up a new spectrum of commercial targets for people used to market analysis, business plans, financial controls and management disciplines. Perhaps more importantly, it made it possible for people to pursue another crucial objective: to move outside the control of others by becoming their own boss.

THE BOARDROOM ALTERNATIVE

Increased public attention on the non-executive director and part-time chairman roles now opens countless company doors to executives who have something to offer in addition to accumulated board experience. The external director concept has generally proved to be sound and receives near-unanimous support.

However, it is difficult for most people to appreciate fully the distinction between the boardroom contribution required of an executive who is running a business and that of a non-executive who operates at arm's length in a semi-supervisory function. Nor is it easy to make an objective assessment of one's own ability to switch from the former to the latter role, especially when the expectations of today's non-executive director are unlikely to mirror perceptions gathered in earlier board experience.

As a result, a high proportion of volunteers, perhaps as many as two-thirds, fail to match the standards set by either a professional non-executive head-hunter or a discerning chairman. It is a fact which continues to disappoint those who consider that any experience as a director or in senior management should ensure an automatic entrée.

THE PART-TIME ROLE

In their hearts, most executives enjoy being in amongst the action; what they do well is planning, organising and getting things done through others. Attempting to confine such talent and energy within the limitations of a series of non-executive boardroom roles is not only unproductive but also generates frustration and conflicts of authority, and usually proves a crass waste of time.

In the absence of a mainstream alternative, many astute minds turned in the direction of the relatively untested multi-role market and found a remarkably receptive response. Ten years ago, when structures were suffering from corporate obesity, it would have been surprising if the notion of 'Senior executive, available now, part time' had raised anything more than a disapproving eyebrow.

Today the scene is quite different, particularly in two types of company.

Firstly, in established small or medium-sized businesses, chief executives and boards realise that continued success is linked to their company's flexibility and speed in meeting ever-changing demands in the design, quality and performance of the products and services it provides. Equally they know that, although these same principles apply to the availability and use of their own management resources, economic forces dictate that they should operate with a lean team and that employing full-time executives is costly. As a result it is not easy to cope with an unexpected upturn in business or the temporary loss of an executive; nor can they readily find someone of calibre with specialist skills either for a short-term assignment or to explore the potential of a new project or market.

The solution, increasingly used, is to draw upon one of the newly formed pools of part-time executive talent available through organisations such as AIC-Inbucon, Executive Stand-By, Future Perfect, Arthur Young's Executive Service or the Institute of Directors' Executive Reserve. On terms which vary from direct employment via appointment fee to executive leasing schemes, these agencies can find people with an amazing range of background skills and experience, including finance, computer systems, marketing, information technology, manufacturing, transportation, exporting, mergers, acquisitions and business management.

As the practice has not only gained acceptance but is often featured in management resource articles – Godfrey Golzen being a knowledgeable initiator – these freelancers are able to promote their own availability with considerable success. They surface repeatedly, substituting for a works manager who is recovering from a heart attack, applying an entrepreneurial mind to exploit dormant assets, making an overseas trading assessment, providing back-up to commercial and technical project teams, opening doors into alternative markets, and in production planning, factory transfer, and legal and company secretarial services. The variety of such opportunities just seems to grow and grow.

Comment

One of the first assignments taken by the Institute of Directors' newly formed service in this field was intimidatingly complex. In summary it read: 'A West German company needs a commercially minded, well-experienced English businessman, who speaks fluent French, to spend six to twelve months establishing a new agency trading base in one of the East African regions.' It took just four weeks to complete!

The second type of company in which part-time executives flourish is the crucial sunrise business, whose director/executive owners have needs which are virtually tailor-made for the part-time executive. In building these enterprises, a disproportionate effort often goes into the relentless drive for growth, to a point when increasing sales assume a false importance and become almost an end in themselves. As the bottom line is sluggish to respond, or turns down, it eventually becomes clear that different management techniques and operating disciplines are necessary. Producing continued growth and profit is difficult enough without trying to anticipate the threats, pressures and opportunities of tomorrow.

Although some companies weather the storms unaided, a rising proportion now look towards the ranks of the seasoned part-time executives for temporary support: for someone who has been there before and who can help set guidelines and apply skills that the company needs today but which, unless available part-time, it could never afford until tomorrow. Financial management and control, information or systems technology, marketing, manufacturing and decisive line executive techniques feature prominently in skills demanded. One day a week is frequently an agreed time input, with duration being left open to subsequent review.

Even though directorship may be discussed, there is often a mutual preference for a trial executive period to see how relationships develop. During a small company's early days the concept of being a director is in any case more notional than real and owners are understandably cautious in offering a boardroom seat, but the invitation and an equity share frequently follow.

LONGER-TERM PROSPECTS

Where will it all lead? There is no guaranteed or failsafe formula for success in business life, but riding a growing trend dramatically improves the odds. The United Kingdom and most of the industrialised western world have passed through two distinct phases. A decade spent forming massive institutional type groups with the maxim 'big is beautiful' was followed by an equal span of confidence-sapping recession.

Now a third phase is under way, dominated by a flexibly minded enterprise culture. As they restructure, shed unwanted activities or realign with competitive forces, companies of all sizes are either voluntarily changing shape and devolving power to smaller autonomous units or are finding that their key people can readily obtain the backing to promote a buy-out as an alternative. Leaving aside sunrise opportunities, there is more than enough happening to whet the appetite of any executives prepared to put their adaptive talents to the test and risk a new style career.

CONSULTING

It is arguable that, even though part-time working at executive level has its own unique features, such activities are only a way of using a consultant at reduced cost. Established consultancies not surprisingly subscribe to a different view. They maintain that their organisations bring to bear a total support-group concept, as against the talents of a single person, and suggest that their performance justifies their not inconsiderable fee differential. Nevertheless, realising that businesses in their embryonic stage neither need nor can handle highly sophisticated presentations, a number have anticipated the opening of a new niche market and have moved into part-time executive leasing.

SUPPLY AND DEMAND

Whether through consultancies or agencies, the processes of matching a still plentiful supply to increasing demand remain laboured. Data sources, or registers, lack polished professionalism and the excessive profit margins for leasing services are frequently a deterrent. Not unlike the early years of other forms of executive recruitment, head-hunting or outplacement, it is a fragmented mini-industry waiting for a bold hand to hammer a dominant image and operating formula into shape.

THE PENDULUM SWINGS

Just as the financial and personal attractions of multi-role careers are becoming recognised, and as more executives are prepared to forsake safe havens for small entrepreneurial or management buy-out challenges, it is ironic that an impending shortage of younger executives means some companies are questioning the wisdom of further reductions in mainstream retirement ages.

Older people may be coming back into fashion. Executives no longer face the prospect of being put out to pasture for almost a quarter of their working lives. Market forces dictated a separate third career phase, and what began almost by necessity is now a way of life. By consensus, part-time activities seem to work well for both individual and company and in many ways prove a more rewarding alternative to the better known non-executive role.

11

Before Joining a Board

Until recently the coming of age for non-executive directors invariably coincided with an impending sixtieth year or when mainstream retirement was clearly in sight. Involvement then continued for ten or more years, frequently with the same company. Whippersnappers in their forties or even fifties were not thought to be sufficiently experienced, mature, acquiescent or available.

These notions predated boardroom shake-outs and the compulsory exodus of senior management. Now perhaps 'life begins at forty' should be the non-executive's maxim as chairmen discount so-called business naïvety in favour of the creative input which flows from busy corporate directors and mainstream executives.

No matter how one assesses age, in the United Kingdom the non-executive function is unquestionably growing. There is consensus that a mixed executive and independent non-executive board brings about better company direction and that all minds broaden in the process. So, as the key elements of demand and supply fit neatly into place, there appears to be something for everyone.

However, the first crucial test of a non-executive director's judgement comes before even joining the board; it is a test of the ability correctly to relate one's own personal qualities to a company's style, board personalities, and expectations of skills and experience. The prospective non-executive, whatever his or her motives for involvement, should examine with due care and diligence the company's credentials, intentions and suitability. Boardrooms seldom contain less than one non-executive who is patently unsuited or who now spends wasteful hours around the table because he or she jumped aboard with great enthusiasm and too little realism. If the matching is wrong, a non-executive is unlikely to add more than a peppercorn of value, or to derive much personal satisfaction from the association.

Those with a non-executive role in mind may care to use the following check lists which draw attention to the crucial stages which precede an appointment.

PERSONAL INTENTIONS

The most frequently identified motives which attract people towards a non-executive role are to:

1. Collect enough non-executive directorships eventually to become a well-paid 'career professional'.
2. Add to a primary business role by expanding interests generally in the belief that they will aid the process of continued personal development.
3. Find something connected with business to help keep occupied during retirement, or to supplement income.
4. Respond to the encouragement of one's own chairman who promotes the use of unrelated non-executives in this and other companies.
5. Act as a paid nominee or business representative of a family, financial or other special interest group.
6. Adopt a multi-role career which may include both part-time chairmanships and non-executive commitments.
7. Support the cause of a good friend who is chairman of a company.
8. Widen knowledge and understanding of corporate governance and the director's role without unduly disrupting an ongoing full-time executive commitment.
9. Follow company tradition by remaining on the board as a non-executive director after retirement.
10. Enjoy the personal challenge of serving on a board which is prestigious and includes sone notable colleagues.

A number of these motives are of questionable value to a company. Some aspiring non-executive directors are so adept in voicing the soundness of their professed motivations that they are quickly able to convince anyone of their good intentions – even themselves.

SUITABILITY

Whatever the motivation, an examination of personal suitability should follow.

Co-directors expect their non-executive directors to have a number of specific personal qualities in addition to experience and skill. Each prospective non-executive should measure his or her capacity to be:

11. An effective and persuasive communicator whose contribution is concise, objective and clear.
12. Socially competent with a deft touch of humour.
13. Independent of mind without prejudicing loyalty to colleagues and the board.
14. A good listener who can focus on key issues and respond with sound advice.
15. Democratic in balancing the interests of shareholders against the interests or others involved with the business.
16. An achiever in his or her own particular chosen field.
17. Constructive in expressing ideas and opinions, even when critical.
18. Able to perform effectively as an individual when divorced from the structure and props of his or her own organisation.
19. Unimpressed by either the prestigious or the financial aspects of the appointment.
20. Positive in making statements and proposals, and unwilling to acquiesce in silence.

It is a matter of deciding not so much whether or not these qualities exist, but whether they are found in sufficient quantities. Objective and honest self-measurement is not easy, but it is crucial before a commitment is made.

KNOWLEDGE

Directors should know their corporate job and understand the range of situations which they may be required to face. To justify existence each non-executive is expected to be a prominent and knowledgeable contributor, especially in areas such as:

21. Verifying the primary objectives and responsibilities of the board in running the business and accurately reporting results both to shareholders and to other interested parties.
22. Understanding directors' personal legal liabilities and the fiduciary requirements of diligence and care.
23. Having the numeracy to interpret accurately the use of key ratios and financial controls.
24. Ensuring the chairman enables the board to function properly and encourages all its members to make a full contribution.
25. Knowing how to address the separate issues of policy, strategy, longer-term business plans and annual budgets.
26. Cutting a sensible and realistic direct path through the vagaries, complexities and influences which bear upon corporate decision making.
27. Planning and making the journey to 'market', either USM or full listing.
28. Determining the best course to take in mergers, acquisitions or divestments.
29. Handling bids and defence action against an unwelcome predator.
30. Supervising the working of audit, remuneration, succession and review committees.

ASSESSING THE COMPANY'S NEEDS

Proper motivations, personal qualities and knowledge may be important but they are of only marginal value unless non-executives understand the company they are to join and feel they can contribute to its needs. To help ensure this a non-executive should:

31. Study the company's last Report and Accounts and, to a lesser extent, its Memorandum and Articles in order to draw conclusions about its possible future health.
32. Know the company's standing in its market, technical and industry sectors.
33. Know where the board intends to direct the company's main activities during the next two or three years – and the reasons why.
34. Have access to the company bankers and auditors.
35. Develop a compatible chemistry with the chairman.
36. Believe a high level of trust, mutual respect and commercial rapport will exist with board colleagues.
37. Have a basic interest in the activities of the company or an affinity with its type of business.
38. Foresee opportunities to use particular skills, knowledge, experience or business connections which may be of value.
39. Accept fully the brief given by the chairman as to how the board functions, the more immediate trials and tribulations which it faces and other proposed changes in its complement or balance.
40. Understand the contribution which is expected by chairman and co-directors.

NON-EXECUTIVE DIRECTORS' SHAREHOLDINGS

Before joining the board of either a private company or a plc, the question of shareholding is sure to be raised. It is an issue which non-executives should be prepared to address.

Purist non-executive directors suggest that holding any shares in a company will sooner or later prove an embarrassment. Pragmatists qualify their comments by size of holding and claim that it is acceptable to hold 'enough, but not enough to matter'. Opportunists follow the philosophy which is natural to them.

Striking a fair balance depends not so much on the rights and wrongs of owning shares, but upon the possible effect their holding may have on a non-executive's independence when contentious board decisions arise which could perhaps lead to a significant change in share values. A recommended benchmark is that the total value of the shareholding, when bought or otherwise received, should not exceed the agreed basic fees that the non-executive will be paid in the coming year. Increments from consulting or other company-related activities, however novel, should be automatically excluded.

Quoted company share values are easily determined, but in private companies the position is quite different. Apart from vagaries in making an initial calculation, once a small equity holding is locked into a private company its value is no more than a figure in the mind of a potential buyer – unless the company comes to market. Considering the sums involved, putting too much stress on the hazards can be misleading because an adequate protective formula coupled to considerable goodwill is invariably extended to a new board member.

Most Articles state that directors are not required to hold any qualification shares. As members of the board they are entitled to receive notice of, to attend and speak at all general meetings of the company. Should incoming non-executives choose to buy shares, they may do so either to show confidence in the company or to enable them to propose or second some specific resolutions at annual general meetings.

COMPANY SCENARIOS

A company's current circumstances, its plans and the status of its board determine the impact of an incoming non-executive. Scenarios abound, and it is impossible to cover the almost infinite variety of situations and relationships which may face a non-executive or to suggest which combination might most influence a decision to join a particular board. One thing is certain: non-executives should probe away until they are satisfied that they understand quite explicitly why their input is being sought. They might be required, for example, to:

- Provide instant management or functional experience to a relatively immature board.
- Inject board disciplines and initiatives to continue current growth and profit.
- Be there simply to add prestige or respectability to the board and, in so doing, attractively window-dress the company on its journey to market.
- Restock the board in the wake of new ownership, internal upheaval or change of chairman.
- Strengthen defences against a suspected predator.
- Join the board as a potential successor to the present chairman.
- Replace an existing non-executive as part of a continuity programme.
- Bring into the boardroom important points of contact or knowledge of specific global functions.
- Appease fractious institutional investors or shareholders.
- Help bring about change and rejuvenation in boardroom strategy and company direction.
- Bolster ability to implement an acquisitive policy.
- Create a better balance of complementary experience between executive and non-executive directors.
- Support a power base or the chairman's politicking.

CONCLUSION

Incoming non-executives may do well to remember that, although some boards are harmonious and fulfilled, this is by no means always the case. People who jump blindly at the chance of a directorship are probably not aware of the difficulties which can beset the role, let alone take stock of their own powers to meet them. It is not unknown for non-executives to be wilfully or unwittingly misled into joining a board. The experienced independents do not agree to join a board until they have applied simple business criteria: they weigh opportunity against limitation, commitment against personal benefit, and risk against reward – the least of which is financial.

One guiding rule remains: if in doubt, don't.

12

Finding and Selecting Non-Executives

A characteristic of searching for a non-executive is that it invariably brings not one but two potential benefits to the hunter. Finding the right body is obviously one. The second, in importance a surprisingly close runner, is the quite revealing insights into the role which result from meeting with people who have expressed enough interest in the appointment to join in exploratory talks. Each discussion helps to clarify the picture of both required input and most likely contributor. These interdependent factors should be neither missed nor neglected.

The sequence leading to the appointment of the non-executive director should be demand led and not supply driven; in fact, the reverse is frequently the norm. Searchers who take the easiest route generally favour amiability and blandness, choosing people who are already known quantities, or prefer to maintain only a vague image of the target in the hope of meeting with an available candidate whose credentials can become an agreed specification. Improved techniques and disciplines are needed in the quest for suitable non-executives who, after all, now represent over a quarter of all plc directors and whose impact on the corporate scene continues to grow.

DEMAND

If demand is allowed to dominate, the following three-step approach may help to increase the probability of making a successful search. It requires the chairman, or the chairman's appointee, to consult with co-directors and to:

1. Draw up a single-page brief which shows;
   - size, complexity and geographical spread of the business;
   - current board members, their roles and primary strengths;
   - key and supportive inputs expected from the incoming non-executive, his or her private company or plc experience, relative skills and knowledge;
   - desired features in the non-executive's personality, style, character, age and chemistry;
   - availability for assignments or mergers and acquisitions activities;
   - scheduled meetings and approximate total time required of the non-executive per year, including homework and travel;
   - level of payment for the position and its likely duration;
   - target appointment date;
   - preferred action route, whether internal or through an external agency.
2. List concise descriptions of non-executive characteristics which everyone is agreed the board does *not* want. This speeds up recognition of non-starters.
3. Note who will act on behalf of the board. Invariably this will be the chairman, but if possible with an existing independent non-executive in support.

The brief's realism should then be checked in a confidential meeting with an outsider, such as:

- A chairman or chief executive friend who is experienced in the use of non-executive directors.
- The head of a consultancy which may have been used on other unrelated work, who understands the company style, and its current activities and objectives.
- A specialist in non-executive director appointments who will know how vital it is to prepare a clear profile. With

half an eye on potential business, such specialists are very willing to display their talents.

Time and cost are both factors which may dictate how a search is carried out and its likely result. Three months from decision to appointment is a practical minimum, but allowing six is ideal; nine months can be regarded as comparative luxury. If all time and related costs are correctly apportioned, handling the appointment internally will be less expensive than using an outside agency, but only marginally so. It is wise to plan six months ahead and to budget the equivalent of a year's fees, although lucky strikes or the acceptance of lower standards may well breach these guidelines.

In some companies the procedure is kept strictly behind the chairman's closed doors, until the future non-executive is introduced just prior to lunch and confirmation of the appointment appears on the agenda. While such imperious action may not guarantee the non-executive's failure, it does indicate an imbalance between the power of the chairman and the rest of the board which augurs ill for the company's fortunes.

Estimates of annual demand vary from one information source to another. Although many smaller companies still do not have non-executive directors on their boards, there are upwards of fifteen thousand non-executive directorships spread amongst companies which have an annual turnover in excess of £3 million. At the present low recycle rate, it is fair to assume about 1,600 new appointments a year. At that level of demand, competition to attract interest from the better performers is understandably quite intense.

SUPPLY

No other sector of the commercial and industrial scene is endowed with so many potential candidates. But at least two out of every three who consider themselves prospective non-executives and join a register or data bank are misguided in so doing. It is better if other board members know of the intention to find a non-executive from the time the subject is first discussed, and if they are asked to contribute in the preparation of a brief. Search progress may be reported from time to time and opinions sought about possibilities, depending on a board's usual 'openness' in such matters. The meeting sequence for prospective people will likely be as follows:

- Chairman and delegated searcher see potentials.
- Chief executive and one non-executive (if existing) see shortlist.
- Other directors meet favoured candidate before a conclusion is drawn. (At this stage the process can, of course, move on to another candidate or go back to square one.)

A vast number of people see the role as one ideally suited to those who are senior industrial and commercial citizens, who have time to spare and who wrongly believe that:

- Any company board or management committee experience constitutes an entry qualification and, if the companies involved were at all sizeable, an automatic graduation.
- Director skills are only an upgraded form of the skills exercised by executive management.
- A non-executive's job is primarily to 'be there' in a generally passive monitoring or counselling capacity.
- The act of volunteering to give something back at low cost to the receiver is an offer companies simply cannot refuse.
- Normal retirement ages do not apply and duration in office is infinite.

They are not alone in such misconceptions. A number of chairmen not only think on similar lines but compound the felony by setting their sights at too modest a level of contribution. Put the two together and the likelihood of making a match of some sort is very high; but the chances of making one which is creditable remain slight, and the evidence of the results is unfortunately to be found in most boardrooms.

Even so, those available still outnumber the opportunities by an enormous margin. The critical issue in supply is quality, and at present quality of supply falls short of demand. Whether or not boards follow a unitary or two-tier format, that situation is unlikely to change.

COMPANY APPOINTMENTS

Chairmen are not only the dominant influence in non-executive appointments but in about 60 per cent of instances they also usually take it upon themselves to find and recommend suitable people. The remaining 40 per cent is split more or less equally between companies using one of the various outside recruitment agencies, brought in at a chairman's instigation, and those forced to accept an appointment imposed by a powerful third party.

When handling the appointment themselves, chairmen have a number of options.

Old boy network

This historical, rather derogatory term simply means making use of friends and any other convenient contact channels through past or current business associations. Still probably the most prolific source of non-executive directors, it is also eminently comfortable to pursue.

> **Comment**
> 'Every competent business executive has sufficient friends to get him on the boards of at least three companies. Friends like to help – use them.'

The above comment is not easy to stomach. Old boy network appointments are sometimes successful, but the practice is addictive and avoids more outright condemnation only because its disasters are relatively easy to cover up. At worst it encourages amiable board sterility and sycophantic politicking.

Professional finger pointing

Bankers, lawyers, accountants, and financial institutions head this list. If pressed, they and many other professional advisers will come up with a name or two from among their more immediate circle. Scope is narrow, and understanding of and relevance to actual need are frequently questionable. Suggestions are nevertheless useful as part of a comprehensive search.

Media chasing

People in the public eye are obvious targets for chairmen who look for competence and credibility as well as for those who like to buy 'trophy' directors. Prominence in business or national affairs usually results in a stream of unsolicited requests to join this, that or the other board. Smitten, sociably minded chairmen will resolutely pursue their prey for months on end, sometimes offering enticing rewards and with little apparent regard to whether notoriety, distinction and charisma are qualities which they should really seek.

> **Comment**
> 'When the chairman joined the meeting it was delightful to see the pride with which he gazed in turn upon each of his assembled colleagues – much as a great hunter might survey big-game trophies lining his study wall. In later years when asked of their value – answer: there was none!'

On the other side of the coin, a favoured tactic is the early and well-publicised announcement of pending change or retirement. A net trawled in this way is seldom hauled up empty.

Scouting

Scouting is certainly the most entertaining of all methods, provided it does not become too frenetic. Luncheons, dinners, seminars and conferences are happy territories to explore, and when a potential quarry comes in view the flow of adrenalin to the predator can be considerable. The eventual face-to-face encounter is sometimes a masterly affair of dual diplomacy. Civilised rejection is a disappointing anti-climax; considered acceptance to further talks, a bright omen.

In-house

Seeking non-executives in-house is easy, and for many retiring executive board members it represents a clear gesture of goodwill from their chairman, who in due course may expect a show of appreciation. A few executive colleagues, apprehensive of outsiders, may welcome the security of knowing of what lies ahead, but most regret a missed opportunity to introduce fresh viewpoints, knowledge and debate. Whereas the other methods do not preclude independence in the non-executive, in this case independence is not even a possibility. Nevertheless in-house appointments remain a regular feature of the majority of boardrooms.

There are inherent weaknesses in all the methods of handling appointments internally: lack of choice, lack of objectivity, lack of assessment experience and the likelihood of convenient alterations to an agreed profile. But the advantages of an experienced chairman handling the project can include: understanding the role and its demands at least as well as many professionals, immediate interaction of style and personal chemistry with prospective non-executives, first-hand briefing on board expectations, and fast, clear decision making about suitability and appointment.

Many of these advantages continue to apply if the task is delegated to perhaps one or two of the current non-executives, but are far less likely to do so if a chairman abdicates responsibility and gives it solely to the chief executive. In that instance, the whole balance of boardroom power is placed in jeopardy.

EXTERNAL AGENCY APPOINTMENTS

Approximately 20 per cent of appointments are credited to the use of agencies in their multifarious forms. Fees do not yet follow any positive commercial pattern, charges from professional search consultants may vary between nothing, for a valued company client, to £20,000. In 1990, recruitment houses, consultants or specialists in this field are charging between £7,500 and £15,000, with PRO NED and IoD being at the lower end of that range. In contrast, Inter-Exec, an organisation which provides career advisory services to fee paying senior executives, does not make any charge to the company. It is a matter for value judgements – the service to choose must surely be the one which gives most help in making the right non-executive selection. Four quite distinct types of agency predominate.

Professional search consultants

These offer a non-executive recruitment service as a limited extension of their mainstream assignment work. This takes the form of a facility either to important corporate clients or to aid the ambitions of valued director contacts who plan to spread their personal interests.

Most of the big names are represented, including Peat Marwick, Korn Ferry, Russell Reynolds, Boyden, Hoggett Bowers, P.A. and Tyzack. Services are highly professional and suited to companies in the top 1,000.

Executive recruitment houses

Most of these have some knowledge of available people as a spin-off from their accumulated executive recruitment files. As non-executive assignments are not part of their normal service a lack of familiarity with the nuances of the subject is understandable. They tend to stick with a recruitment pattern established when selecting front runners for executive positions – which is exactly the approach *not* needed: each cobbler to his last.

It is worth remembering that even in their natural habitat, search and executive recruitment consultancies achieve a successful rate of only around the 70 per cent mark. They are unlikely to do better with non-executives.

Non-executive director appointment consultants

Having been around for a number of years without achieving prominence, increased publicity for the non-executive role has now improved their presence in the market-place. However, few carry out more than twenty assignments annually – a benchmark below which it is an unrewarding struggle to continue the process of gathering information and keeping enough top-flight contacts to form a powerful and versatile portfolio. The alternative, dependence upon a high proportion of volunteers is an unsatisfactory limitation, although some of these consultants do an effective job.

Specialist appointment services

Although only two in number, these carry out almost half of all external agency assignments and therefore warrant individual description.

The Promotion of Non-Executive Directors (PRO NED) was founded in 1982 and is sponsored by the Accepting Houses Committee, the Bank of England, the British Institute of Management, the Committee of London and Scottish Clearing Bankers, the Confederation of British Industry, Equity Capital for Industry, the Institutional Shareholders

Committee, Investors in Industry Group plc and the Stock Exchange.

Starting from scratch and providing a literally free service, it was never going to be easy for PRO NED. Additionally, there was much use of a type of 'computerised sausage-machine' concept, whereby a company's requirement would be fed into a computer, which then churned out a list of names. The dangers of this are obvious: too great a reliance on the emerging list as the sole source of ideas, coupled with a dependence on the quality of the original data which, when PRO NED began, was poor. Had it not been for the creative guidance of David Walker, the selfless pioneering work by Jonathan Charkham and, until his decision to leave in 1989, a quite exceptional contribution from Douglas Strachan, the organisation might already be dead and buried. Instead it gathers pace from year to year, bound by the collective wisdom of its establishment sponsors and keeping a balance between its twin objectives of 'promoting use' and 'supplying suitable bodies'.

With nationwide meetings supported by a host of leading industrialists and backed with a series of clear, concise and well-presented booklets and survey reports, PRO NED has hit its plc targets with great effect. As a result about four in every five of their assignments come from that sector. Now the agency is wisely spreading the net to attract a higher proportion of medium and smaller private companies.

Each company's non-executive need is met by a selection process which uses a vast computerised store of available people. Many of those listed, including many women, are executives on file at the instigation of their chairmen, who both agree with the non-executive principle and find that their executives benefit from the time spent on the board of an unrelated company.

Matching non-executive to company remains the crucial element. Within the existing concept, everyone acknowledges that making a match is not and never will be an exact science, or even always close enough to avoid some adverse comment. Without recourse to a stronger search element, sheer weight of numbers will not always correct the imbalances any such data-reliant system will throw up. Having made over four hundred appointments, however, PRO NED is able to provide an impressive list of client companies and candidates, many of whom have international experience, fees are now charged.

The second specialist agency is IoD Board Appointments, run by the Institute of Directors. About twenty years ago Sir Maurice Dean first gave words of sound advice to chairmen and pointed a discriminating finger in the direction of useful non-executive additions to their boards. Steady if unspectacular growth in the organisation followed for over a decade, and when PRO NED came on the scene continued independence, as against merger or association, found mutual favour.

The twin objectives of promotion and supply are shared with PRO NED. However methods differ in some areas. For example, in the Institute of Directors service:

- Greater emphasis and time is said to be given to the study of each company's existing board formation, strengths and weaknesses before drawing up assignment details. Smaller company chairmen frequently need guidance, and the IoD tries to provide this.
- Numbers of people on record as 'availables' are lower, although any such computerised process is likely to encourage rapid expansion.
- Selection is supplemented by search and shortlists are shorter.
- Part-time chairman appointments are featured.
- Promotional activities are weaker than those of PRO NED and tend to centre around membership publications.
- The service is open to all companies, whether or not their directors are members of the Institute of Directors (although most outsiders do not know).

The Institute of Directors, as a result, is perceived to be closer to the needs of private companies, who make up two-thirds of clients. The service attracts considerable numbers of chairmen who for the first time are exploring the possible use of non-executive directors on their board.

Assignments take longer, between six and twelve weeks, but achieve a better than average strike rate and now include many non-executives with European or US connections.

When drawing conclusions on the scope and relative value of the various agency services a chairman should also consider these questions:

- Do we have a policy on non-executive recruitment and does it work? If not, accepting the importance of a board appointment, can we afford to risk not using an external agency?
- Should we go for limited agency support as a check and balance to our own searches or for a total service?
- Are we in a global market-place, with the Single European Market and overseas expansion in mind? Should we look for someone with relative international experience, perhaps a foreign national, and how can an agency help?
- Which type of agency appears to best understand and suit our size, style and particular need?
- If we give an agency the go-ahead, are we all of a mind to see it through or will we just procrastinate?
- Are we genuinely prepared to discuss our board affairs openly with an outsider – even in confidence?

The last point raises an interesting recurring question for it is often difficult to make disclosures concerning internal board friction, shortfalls in performance, indecision about the future, and fears of a power-seeking colleague or an external predator. In addition, some companies talk in urgent terms then back away, usually reflecting a general state of indecisiveness within the boardroom. Chairmen resort to dressing up real needs in a variety of guises, hedging the awkward issue or limiting the information supplied on the pretext of lack of time.

These undercurrents seldom surface until a shortlist is put forward and the need to respond brings matters to a head. Then a period of silence follows as dissenting factions line up their support forces and real power issues are put on the table. In such instances a reasonable betting man could lay high odds against any appointment being made. For a time perhaps some board members might have seen an incoming non-executive as a mediator or, worse still, a healer of all ills – which of course a non-executive is not.

FORCED-CHOICE APPOINTMENTS

The final 20 per cent of non-executives arrive at the board table via an almost forced-choice arrangement. As we saw in Chapter 8, nominees may be representatives of minority groups, particular shareholdings, investors, employees or other interested parties who have the power to influence board decisions. Appointees of sizeable debenture holdings can be said to have a useful watching brief role on behalf of their masters but, as in the ill-fated case of De Lorean, they may not serve with great distinction. The titles non-executive director or part-time in house consultant are popular ways of describing someone leveraged on to a board to see that certain policies are followed and, regardless of any line management structure, to have a direct say in which executive does what, when and how.

Forward-thinking financial institutions, banks and regulating bodies moved a step away from more obvious forms of coercion when they opted to sponsor PRO NED. One of the key reasons for its very existence was in order to be the recipient of company chairmen, perhaps nudged in its direction because it was thought their boards could benefit from the wider use of outside directors.

Comment

'Having long since retired, the quite aged founding father and majority owner maintained a discreet distance from the board. He attended annually as a non-executive director.

Between these visits the board went about its business, but with one significant difference. After each meeting the chairman

> went to the old boy, reported the board's deliberations and decisions and asked for approval. Later the chairman returned to his co-directors armed with the real board's instructions – and a revised set of minutes'.

Coercion in any degree impinges upon freedom of choice and a board's ultimate responsibility, but its existence is a fact of business life: some so-called non-executive directors, or their shadows, have undue power or leverage to determine a company's direction. That situation will alter only as fast as either human nature changes or companies adopt a system which places representatives on a board which is designed to accommodate their supervisory role but which also keeps them at arm's length and prevents them from interfering in meetings of operational executive directors.

It would be a real bonus if such a system, perhaps of two boards, also allowed much of the character, style and interest of original ownership to be retained through non-executive membership of a separate board, so leaving full-time executives with greater freedom to run the business.

WHAT TO PAY A NON-EXECUTIVE

Enough, but not enough to matter is the golden rule. When a non-executive is there for the money, independence is in jeopardy.

Attempts to relate non-executive levels of payment to that of a chairman lack consistency because the latter's time demands are not only greater but are liable to fluctuate from year to year. The problem is compounded because the more effective chairmen usually receive higher than average pay, although devoting the same number of days, or even fewer, to the job. Similarly, linking pay to a chief executive produces its own set of anomalies. Although it can be assumed that the chief executive's basic remuneration will reflect a company's size and complexity, the range between small private companies and major groups is just too wide to draw sensible conclusions.

Payment of non-executives is best determined on its own merits. In medium-sized companies the average is currently about £8,000 for a total time input of some twenty days a year. The range is wide, from £5,000 to £15,000, with only a small percentage above or below. In smaller companies, where any boardroom fee costs are viewed with alarm, sums of a more modest nature are usually agreed, at least initially.

What a non-executive is paid no longer ranks as confidential information. The best way for a chairman to get an accurate picture is to check historical trends from recently published surveys, then talk about today's figures with other chairmen, perhaps a pay consultant, and the people who run IoD Board Appointments or PRO NED who both have up-to-date information.

A median figure, when established, may need adjustment to take into account payment variations between one non-executive director and another. There is no good reason why all non-executives should be paid the same or all be required to agree a uniform time commitment. It is desirable, and not uncommon, to use certain non-executives for committee or assignment work.

The sums can easily be worked out. One method is to take 40 per cent of the median payment as a reward for basic board responsibility, 365 days a year, and 60 per cent related to the time element. For example, if twenty days at the median level is equal to £8,000, then sixteen days would represent around £7,000 and twenty-eight days would be around £10,000. A commitment much under sixteen or over twenty-eight days is stretching the non-executive concept: one to the point of not being able to play any meaningful part outside scheduled meetings, the other to the point of being too involved, if not a nuisance.

Payment is far from an exact science; figures are usually rounded up and reviews are made annually, even if no change results. Attempts to be precise about times and payments should be avoided – it is a penny-pinching exercise which is not in keeping with accepted non-executive commitment philosophy. If and when irregularities in time demands do occur which warrant some change in payment, they are best dealt with on a retrospective basis.

Apart from reimbursement of expenses, further payments should be taboo. That means no company performance-related bonus, no share options, and no perks, pensions or inducements which may place independence at risk. The same ban is recommended for any form of contract other than a mutual understanding, confirmed in the chairman's board-approved letter of invitation. The invitation may state that an initial term of three years is expected, possibly extending to six, subject to an annual review between chairman and non-executive.

Terms of engagement, together with the key points to be discussed between chairman and non-executive *before* appointment is made, are shown at the end of the next chapter as part of a Code of Practice.

13

Liabilities, Information and Code of Practice

In the United States, prospective non-executive directors would be out of character if, before joining a board, they failed to ask three stock questions:

- Does the company provide Directors and Officers insurance?
- Is there an audit committee?
- Do the non-executives form a majority on the board?

Unless the answers to all three were affirmative, the company would probably have either to look elsewhere or to conform to what is now generally accepted US practice.

In the United Kingdom almost the reverse applies:

- Companies may be in default if they provide blanket liability insurance cover for directors, although this position will shortly change. Alternative private individual cover is available, but take-up is low.
- A lethargic approach to self-regulation leaves audit committees an almost endangered species except in larger plcs.
- Executive directors still rule the roost, both in power and numbers.

The fact that UK companies do not conform to established practice on the other side of the Atlantic, or Channel for that matter, does not necessarily mean they are wrong. However, in all these instances there is growing support for the view that they are not right.

Insurance, being primarily defensive, is of questionable importance except that lack of it inclines many directors towards uncomfortable silence. Regulation loosely framed is loosely interpreted. During the past forty years an increasing number of UK company directors have acted in ways which show scant regard for either voluntary regulation or normal standards of ethical practice. Executives who dominate a board can, if they choose, run rings around a brace of unwary non-executive colleagues.

Audit committees and an independent non-executive majority will not in themselves change the corporate world, but both have the advantage of operating within the boardroom circle, and sooner or later that is where regulation has to penetrate.

THE NEW ACTS

High hopes accompanied the introduction of the 1985–6 Companies and Insolvency Acts, which laid down quite exacting professional standards to be expected of boards and individual directors. These hopes have been slow in coming to fruition, but in fairness the task of changing some director attitudes towards personal or corporate responsibilities was never expected to be easy. Ignoring any form of regulation, they weave a web of deals and arrangements which conceal reasonable proof of wrongful action and frustrate the levying of due penalties. The first five thousand or so reported insolvency cases produced proceedings against few more than three hundred directors. Significantly, however, over 90 per cent of the cases concluded have resulted in an order for disqualification.

Theoretically, a director now has to face a formidable list of almost three hundred possible offences, the more popular models being described in a variety of publications, including the Institute of Directors' *Guide to Boardroom Practice* compiled by Andrew Hutchinson. In fact, such a battery of constraints and punishments should not strike fear and trepidation into the hearts of non-executives. A majority clearly apply themselves to the job, allowing their thoughts and actions to be governed only by a creditable sense of right and wrong. A significant minority are nevertheless prepared to hide behind a veil of ignorance or have an aversion to acknowledging the rules until trouble looms. Then it is time for a rapid exodus accompanied by the usual protestations of innocence.

The Acts are not, in fact, aimed primarily at non-executives. (For a comprehensive listing of offences and penalties under the Companies Act 1985, the Insolvency Act 1986, and related legislation, see Appendix I of *Directors' Personal Liabilities*, IoD, 1988.) They share five quite simple objectives. These are to:

- Clarify the ground rules as they relate to present-day company procedures.
- Create greater awareness of the standards expected of a company director.
- Give confidence to the diligent, who act in good faith and with care and skill.
- Deter or straighten those with an inclination to deviate from correct behaviour.
- Provide justification to catch and punish the wilful wrongdoers.

The requirement to act with honesty and in good faith is the same for both full-time executive and non-executive, but in practice the application of diligence and skill carries a degree or two of leeway for the non-executive. The intention is to differentiate between what might be expected of a qualified professional or expert, say a full-time executive director responsible for overseas contracts or process engineering, and a non-executive with only general appreciation of the subjects.

But, by the same token, competence in corporate governance, numeracy and awareness of a director's proper duty are skills which every non-executive is expected to have in full measure – after all, the ability to exercise those skills is among the primary reasons for the non-executive's existence. Experience shows that a company which runs into trouble invariably does so because its board has been unaware of the company's true position, has failed to look ahead and has not recognised the pitfalls *en route*.

When the bell tolls, it is unconvincing for bolting non-executives to suggest, as many do, that liquidators cannot hold them personably liable because they had nothing to do with running the company. As directors, they had everything to do with directing how the company was to be run and ensuring that an agreed plan was properly carried out – including the penetration of smokescreens thrown up to cover operational indecision or incompetence – no matter how dominant in numbers the executive may be.

INFORMATION

Corporate tragedies can often be traced back to abysmal communications within both board and top management. Ironically enough, awareness failures are not exclusive to quill-pen administrations; they are to be found in companies which in other spheres of business already use computer services capable of providing the board with all the electronic wonders of information technology.

Inherent information weakness and the potential of IT has resulted in a number of boards giving communications a definitive role and including that responsibility in the brief of either one of their executive members or the company secretary. This upsurge in prominence for a pivotal communications officer seems infinitely sensible and, if it generates information in fresh, imaginative form, countless minds around UK board tables will at last be liberated from the burden of interpreting events through reams of mesmeric documents based on stereotyped accounting practice.

It is perhaps fair to say that no other country in the world is as saturated with accountants, qualified or otherwise, as the United Kingdom. There are 150,000, two-thirds of whom work in commercial and industrial firms – more than the total in all the other countries which form the European Community. Apart from handling matters of pure finance, accountants are caught between being recorders of a company's numerical history and being its sole source of regular board information. So often they interpret the role as a need to circulate a cascade of figures, segregated, detailed, running along inflexible channels and too repetitive to allow absorption let alone action. They are on a time-consuming treadmill of diminishing value to both producers and recipients. How different the fortunes of UK companies might have been if blessed to saturation point with 100,000 creative commercial marketeers!

In the absence of suspicious circumstances, non-executives are entitled to believe that information provided for them is honestly prepared. However, with their assumed boardroom know-how and experience, they are expected to be fully aware of the timeliness, accuracy, provision and not least the security of important information. In boardrooms, as in law, ignorance is no excuse.

Keeping people informed about the company necessitates a constant flow of fact and opinion, most of which is subject to board approval. There are three kinds of document which are of particular importance:

- The cumulative records, knowledge, forecasts and opinions, sourced company wide, from which board information is distilled and upon which its considerations and decisions are likely to be based.
- The records or minutes of board meetings which must be held for inspection by the auditors and, if necessary, by insolvency practitioners. Minutes record an agreed, albeit distilled, version of what was said by directors, the conclusions drawn and the decisions taken. From that evidence directors may be judged as to whether or not they knew or should have known what was happening. Did they act or should they have acted? Did they care and use adequate skill in caring?
- External circulars such as interims or annual Report and Accounts, prospectus, defence or predatory statements,

and a wealth of similar material which covers what is publicised or said outside the boardroom. Did the directors fully understand what was written? Did they have enough factual evidence to support those statements?

Verification

Any non-executive who is conscious of possible information gaps should carry out the salutary exercise of reading through a batch of lawyer's verification notes. There is a fairly standard list of questions asked of all directors when important issues are at stake, for example in the preparation of a prospectus. Their answers provide a formal record that statements which express fact or opinions are not only correct but do not contain inferences which could in any way mislead a reader.

Each director is required to check and approve the notes to signify acceptance of responsibility for the accuracy of information provided, as well as the honesty with which it is given. These headings illustrate their breadth:

- Personal credentials, interests, shareholding, contract and payment.
- Working capital and cash flow forecasts.
- Current trading patterns, recent trends or changes.
- Trading expectations; optimistic or pessimistic statements which have or are now being made.
- Share option schemes and pension safeguards.
- Form and function of subsidiary companies.
- Company premises.
- Material contracts.
- Investments, acquisitions and divestments over the past three years.
- Current or outstanding litigation and arbitration.

Obviously the finance director and company secretary have major roles to play in the presentation, use and safety of the company's property, of which information is part. Once again these stringent legal obligations highlight the value of having people with independence of mind and status in both those functions.

It is exaggerating the point to suggest that non-executive directors know all there is to know about everything – and all the time. It is none the less remarkable how, like a hangman's noose, the process of reading through verification notes helps concentrate the mind: asking questions is never again considered as just an obligatory routine.

Information for non-executive director orientation

To help bring a non-executive on-stream quickly there are two steps related to information which a chairman can take:

- Between a non-executive's acceptance of an appointment and his or her first meeting, the chairman can arrange a programme of company familiarisation, which includes briefing sessions from the chairman, chief executive, finance director and company secretary.
- Prior to each of the subsequent three meetings, if not already standard practice, non-executive and chairman should arrange to talk through at some length the board agenda and matters which relate to it.

Presenting non-executive information

It is incongruous that when annual Report and Accounts invariably show each executive director's function, and of course that of the chairman, readers are obliged to accept that non-executives are adequately described by the use of an asterisk or some such abstract notation alongside their name.

As non-executives account for one-quarter of plc directors and almost the same proportion in medium or large private companies, it is not unreasonable for the reader to expect some pertinent information to be circulated as quickly as possible about each new member of this influential body of people. Such information might include the reason for being invited to join the board, background, significant achievements and other current activities. This should be shown in the first company Report and Accounts after appointment, and subsequently updated each third year if the non-executive's name is for re-election.

A more contentious issue, but no less important, is the need for a company to disclose the origins of its non-executives in all Report and Accounts, prospectuses and similar documents. Definitions of their source may be restricted to one of the following options:

- Ex-chairman.
- Ex-Chief executive.
- Ex-executive director.
- Independent.
- Professional non-executive.
- Nominee.
- Representative, suitably qualified by: debenture holder, investor, employee, shareholder or family.
- Ex-professional adviser to the company.

These two quite simple ways of disclosing and presenting each non-executive's personal information and origins would not only present a clear indication of how a board is constructed, but also provide a fascinating insight into the board strategy and the style of its chairman or chief executive. For these reasons alone, however, both suggestions could meet stiff resistance.

CODE OF PRACTICE

The Code, which I originally produced in an IoD booklet in 1982, is intended to focus attention on a number of key points which have a direct bearing on a non-executive's role and the way in which it is to be carried out. They are best discussed and agreed between chairman and non-executive at the time an invitation to join the board is being extended and accepted.

The Code is primarily for the guidance of a non-executive who is independent. However, the principles apply equally to all non-executives since many of the important factors which affect their role and terms of appointment are often still loosely interpreted or even subject to fundamental misconception.

1. The non-executive has met the other members of the unitary, two-tier or twin boards and is conversant with the financial status, business situation and objectives of the company.
2. The non-executive is independent and does not have:

   (a) a contractual connection with the company other than the office of director, or any involvement with the company, its directors or management which could affect the exercise of independent judgement;
   (b) a relationship which may stem from prior executive responsibilities, association with the company's professional advisers, or the representation of financial institutions, major shareholders or various sectional interests.

3. All areas, where a conflict of interests may arise, have been noted and found acceptable by both the individuals and companies concerned.
4. The main purpose and thrust of the non-executive's individual contribution has been identified together with the nature of any special assignments or participation in audit, succession, remuneration and other committees.

   It is recognised that four of the primary contributions of all non-executive directors are to:

   (a) expand the horizons within which the board determines the strategy of its business and to bring into such discussions particular knowledge, experience or skills which are relevant and which the board may otherwise lack;

(b) watch how the board functions and, through the chairman, propose any changes which may seem necessary;
(c) improve the decision-making quality of the board;
(d) monitor executive performance against agreed objectives.

5. The chairman will ensure the board directs the company through the medium of rational and constructive discussion at properly constituted meetings.
6. The non-executive will take an active part in board deliberations and accepts the legal responsibility to act bona fide, with due diligence and care, in the interests of the company as a whole and in parity with executive directors.

   In this context the term 'interests of the company' embraces its relationships with and the interests of all employees, suppliers, customers and shareholders.
7. The non-executive either has or, within reasonable time, will have acquired:

   (a) a sound knowledge of the nature and extent of the business;
   (b) an awareness of the economic, political and social environment in which the business is conducted;
   (c) an understanding of the availability of financial resources and the levels of current or proposed investments;
   (d) an acquaintance with the senior people responsible for the company's operational management.

8. In addition to the regular provision of adequate financial information, the non-executive directors' common-law right of access to information needed to perform their duties is fully acknowledged, and this availability is ensured.
9. If the company does not have an audit committee as such, the independent non-executive directors may, at their discretion, meet separately with the auditors at least once a year.

10. The non-executive's primary intention is clearly to make an objective and constructive contribution towards the effective direction of the company's affairs. Such intention implies working within the framework of the board to resolve conflicts of opinion, personality or policy.

It is, however, understood that the non-executive director may take such individual action, including resignation, as he or she considers the company's interest demands if:

(a) the board persists in a course of action which is believed to be contrary to the 'interests of the company';
(b) the board will not take steps to correct what are believed to be unacceptable irregularities within the company.

In both instances, the points at issue will have been previously raised and discussed during one or more scheduled meetings of the board at which the non-executive has attended and made his or her opinions known.

11. An approximate annual time commitment and a rate of remuneration, subject to review, have been noted and these fully take into account the nature and scope of the non-executive director's anticipated contribution.
12. Length of service as a non-executive director with the company is expected to be for an initial term of three years which may, if mutually agreed, be extended up to a total of six years but is unlikely to exceed that duration.
13. Termination of service as a director may be given at any time, by either party, without implied compensation to the non-executive or to the company.
14. At least once each year the chairman and non-executive will carry out a critical in-depth review of board performance and the non-executive's personal contribution.

14

The Non-Executive Role: Concluding Observations

This chapter takes the form of a series of comments and reflections on the role of the non-executive.

- In spite of all the ostensible impersonations there is no such being as an archetypal non-executive.
- Although the principles underlying a non-executive's *raison d'être* remain consistent, in practice the role is subject to immeasurable variations according to the size, nature and circumstances of both board and company. On occasions a non-executive's task may seem like that of the Dublin barman so aptly described by Kieran Cooke in the *Financial Times* as 'one able to dispense ten drinks, hold four conversations, order a taxi, put a bet on a horse, make a sandwich, throw out a troublesome customer, wash glasses and wipe the top of the bar, all at the same time, and in a crowd that would frighten the hardiest rush-hour commuter'.
- There is still a sufficient number of mediocre non-executive performances to fuel cynical attitudes towards the role and its 'jobs for the boys' connotation. The reasons for such inadequacy are likely to lie in a non-executive being unsuitable, unused, over-committed, related, nominated, aligned, opportunistic, of dubious intent or just in the wrong board concept.
- Although it is important for non-executives to be good communicators who can judge when and how to make a point, and then do it well, many long-surviving non-executives owe their existence to no more than an

impressive bearing and plausible ambiguity.

- What a non-executive has to offer is a perishable commodity, and it is always prudent to remember the sell-by date.
- 'Non-executive director' is frequently a convenient catch-all title used to embrace nominees, misnomers, mismatches and mistakes. It only begins to have board significance when prefixed by the word 'independent'.
- If the Code of Practice recommended in Chapter 13 is sound, one must accept that, in spite of current suggestions to the contrary, the majority of non-executive directors cannot genuinely be described as independent.
- The presence of non-executives on a board may suggest propriety but in no way constitutes a guarantee. The lack of individual accountability in the role can either deny honourable contributors their accolade or provide shadow enough for clever imposters to lurk with safety.
- People within a company and those outside who have, or may have, interests in it now expect to be better informed about its non-executive directors, their background, current status, degree of independence and reasons for appointment – at the very least through information published in the annual Report and Accounts.
- Two objectives of the 1985–6 Acts were to deter wrongdoing or negligence by a single director or a board in concert through joint and several liability, and to encourage professionalism in director skills leading to more effective self-regulation. Five years on, identifying wrongdoers is still no easy task and making successful prosecutions even less so. One possible measure is that, if a non-executive is seen to quit a company when trouble looms, his or her 'licence' to act again in that capacity should be withdrawn through the issue of an appropriate version of the Bank of England's 'Fit and Proper' letter.
- The first test of non-executive's judgement comes in deciding which board to join and which to reject.
- As in most endeavours, optimum effectiveness is achieved only when all the key related factors are right. For non-executive directors this means the character and role of

the chairman and the chief executive, the composition of the board, the opportunity to contribute and the non-executive's own character and abilities. The fact that this ideal fusion seldom happens is no reason to lower objective standards.

- Promoters of the non-executive cause are not helped by some company chairmen. Their inadequacy in non-executive selection and use is clearly reflected in disappointing performance.
- PRO NED and the Institute of Directors Appointments Service are established leaders in non-executive director recruitment and can boast an impressive list of client companies. They would deny their founding objectives if the price put on their services were to be allowed to rise beyond the reach of small companies, co-operatives, or the like, whose chairmen are, for the first time, trying to find a non-executive.
- The need for non-executives depends largely on the company concerned. Non-executives should be currently active businessmen or women, or have some important specialist background. There is not much value in the statement that they are there to represent shareholders because non-executives have no effective constituency with shareholders unless appointed by a shareholders' group. Chairmen and boards of directors are violently opposed to such appointments, viewing them as unwarranted interference.
- In management buy-outs it is the buyers who have access to most of the know-how required to judge a company's present and potential value. It is the independent non-executives who must ensure that all relevant information is published and available to existing and prospective shareholders, and they must act in their best interests when recommending a bid response.
- Companies are only nominally owned by their shareholders. Directors decide where they wish to take the company and how it is going to get there; owners are then invited to pay for the ride – until, that is, another invitation lands on the table in the form of a bid.

- While mindful of their shareholders' interests, non-executives also need to remember that the role of business in society is far wider than just the production or sale of commodities.
- Face-to-face working contact between non-executive director and both chief executive and finance director is essential if non-executives are to understand fully the company tempo and how it operates. European two-tier concepts block this creative or critical access; a British system need not necessarily suffer the same disadvantages.
- 'Two tiers' indicates the superiority of one tier and the subservience of the other. Even though executives may have 95 per cent of territorial advantage and possession, it is the totally non-executive supervisory board which takes the crucial decisions. Twin-boards, on the other hand, share a unifying bond of total responsibility.
- In its own quiet way, a twin-board system seems to solve many of a boardroom's more volatile and contentious issues. It recognises that, although executive and policy boards have quite different functions, they are equal and should work in unison not isolation. By including the chief executive and finance director on both the policy and executive boards an important link is retained, while a critical mass of independent non-executives are able to enjoy a close working relationship with the chief executive and finance director.
- Opting for either a two-tier or twin-board system does not mean that the appointment of employee representatives as worker directors will necessarily follow; that remains a matter of company policy.
- It is not mere coincidence that some companies or groups always seem to find themselves in areas of opportunity while others are still trying to survive in yesterday's business. The cause is found in the leadership, quality, ability and work ethic of their respective boards.
- Directors of British companies, used to executive dominance in the boardroom, cannot allow habit to frustrate changes in board structures. In a complex environment the quality of direction must be raised if a board is to

serve its company well and also meet the cultural and ethical standards now expected by society.

Ultimately, each non-executive has to be his or her own judge. Answering these questions may help.

Do I:

Feel comfortable with my motives for becoming a non-executive director?
Understand fully the non-executive role?
Know what the company expects of me?
Have the experience, knowledge, skills and ability to meet those expectations?
Have both the time and resolution to contribute?

Can I:

Relate to and work with the personalities involved: is the chemistry right?
Be effective within the board's operating style and structure?
Retain my independence and ability to act without prejudice?

Will I:

Benefit from this association and experience?
Recognise when it is time to go?

Perhaps the final word may be allowed to go to Sir Peter Thompson, chairman of National Freight Corporation, who said of the decision to privatise NFC with or without its loss-making National Carriers Division (*The Independent on Sunday*, 18 February 1990):

> I am about to describe what could have been my biggest mistake – which thanks to the wisdom of our non-executive directors, I was not allowed to make . . . They argued that if we were not prepared to privatise NFC as a whole, maybe the government would take the view that we should sell off the profitable parts and leave us to manage the rump . . . I was obdurate. They were adamant and they (the non-executives) outnumbered me . . . How wrong I was and how right they were . . . *Vive* non-executive directors.

Index